MISSION
— TO —
MILLION$

TAKING BIG IDEAS AND MAKING THEM REALITY

ELIZABETH FRISCH

Author: Elizabeth Frisch
Title: Mission to Million$
ISBN: 978-1-77204-121-7
Category: BUSINESS & ECONOMICS/General

Publisher:
Black Card Books™
Division of Gerry Robert Enterprises Inc.
Suite 214 5-18 Ringwood Drive
Stouffville, Ontario
Canada, L4A 0N2
International Calling: 1-647-361-8577
www.blackcardbooks.com

MISSION
— TO —
MILLION$

TAKING BIG IDEAS AND MAKING THEM REALITY

ELIZABETH FRISCH

ACKNOWLEDGMENTS

This book would never have happened without the thousands of clients who provided me data over the years, shared their ideas, bared their souls and vented their frustrations. They also willingly (and occasionally grudgingly) mastered the practices taught in this book, even when they had every reason to quit and go back to a more comfortable place in this world.

I want to first acknowledge you, my idea leaders (yes, that is *you*, if you picked up this book). You have the powerful vision, you just don't know how to make your idea happen—or maybe you've hit a wall. You may be stuck, frustrated, worn-out, burnt-out...just fill in the blank _____. You are still in the game and trying to move forward. I acknowledge your struggle, and am committed to giving you a pathway to success!

To my husband, Mike, my kids, William and Ally, my mom and dad (miss you!) and my best friend, Scottie: Thank you for always challenging me to be the person in this world I only dreamed I could be, and for supporting me through crazy hours, late nights, difficult conversations, and my oft-absence as I wandered the world and figured all of this out.

To my muses at the United States Green Building Council (USGBC), both past and present; you inspire and support me, and let me help you play a huge game in the world. You were the ones who told me to write this book so more people like you could have a tool in their tool belt to make big ideas happen. Thank you for your idea leadership. And thank you for being willing to follow my practices, testing all my theories to their absolute limits, and for changing the world one community at a time. I sleep better at night knowing my childrens' healthy future lies in your hands.

Finally, to the men and women who serve in our armed forces and the civilians who serve you. From the first day I was hired to work with you, I was struck with how much you could take on. You have limited resources, impossible tasks and insurmountable odds that would make most people run the opposite direction, yet you make ideas happen. Thank you for your sacrifice and service to our country.

TO MY READERS AND IDEA LEADERS

Here in your hands lies the path forward to your idea. Feel the freedom, relief, and energy flowing back into you...all walls are coming down...

This is my gift to you.

Now go and build that idea into reality.

With much love, admiration, and respect,

Elizabeth Frisch

TABLE OF CONTENTS

INTRODUCTION

THE POWER OF MAKING AN IDEA HAPPEN

"The energy of the mind is the essence of life."

- Aristotle (translation from The Metaphysic)

How many times throughout the day do you have an idea? How many times do you fail to take any action on your ideas? How many times have you failed to make a great idea happen? Yet, how many of you remember every time you did make some idea happen in your life, your work, or your community? Do you remember the energy, joy, elation, and happiness that flowed with it? Even when it was hard, it was worth it.

This book is for people who want lives filled with energy from seeing more of their ideas happen and succeed. This book is for people who may have failed in making some big idea, dream, or change happen, and are still seeking a way to make it happen. This book is for people who need to learn that no matter where they came from, who they know, or where they sit in some hierarchy, becoming an idea leader is achievable for everyone. This book is for those who want to see how others succeeded in achieving their dreams and to learn from their life lessons. Finally, this book is for everyone who wants clear, actionable steps and a framework they can use over and over again for advancing ideas both big and small at work, at home, and in their communities.

Mission to Million$ is Book 1 of my 3-book series on *Empowering People Into Leadership*. *Mission to Million$* focuses on teaching you how to train yourself and your mind into lifetime habits. You will need to master these habits to be successful in taking big ideas and making them a reality consistently, no matter how long it takes, and no matter what circumstances life throws at you. Reading this book will give you a clear understanding of why you currently may be stuck in a paradigm that causes you to lose and/or fail at implementing your ideas. You will also learn a powerful new 'Idea Growth' framework to permanently break your bad habits!

You will accomplish this by learning eight practices that I have observed over and over again and seen used by thousands of people from all walks of life who have succeeded in making big ideas happen. You'll hear a variety of stories from people who have been there. These stories are as diverse as the ideas themselves; you'll find common themes in their experiences.

The practices taught in this book can be used by people in either established or start-up organizations. I have successfully taught and used these methods in organizations large and small, implementing ideas from a group of a dozen people, to ideas impacting hundreds of thousands of people. The practices shared in this book are very specific; they address the behaviors that can support us or sabotage us in getting our ideas out into the world. Each practice can be adapted and used based on what your idea is, and on the types of people and organizations you are working with.

How did I get on the path of Idea Leadership?

I am a self-declared recovering chemical engineer. I entered my own self-imposed 12-step program to achieve balance in my brain about 12 years ago. It began with the birth of William, my first child, and continued when my daughter Ally was born. Until that time, I labored under the illusion (or delusion, as some would call it) that I could engineer the world. If I built the system solidly enough, it would hold when humans failed. To a degree that can be true (as my engineer friends point out to me). But, when my beautiful, wonderful children joined this world, they taught me very quickly that the best systems, technologies, and controls are not worth a crap if human beings don't support them. It became painfully clear to me that I was working from the wrong direction and mindset, not just in my parenting, but in my business and my personal relationships.

So, after spending seven years as an engineer, auditor, project manager, performance analyst and business builder, I decided to focus solely on the intersection of traditional business performance approaches and the psychology of the human mind. I learned how the mind has to be engaged to shift behavior to drive sustained performance.

In 2002, after spending several years cross-training to learn to use the right side of my brain, I opened my first consulting firm. My very first project was at one of the largest military installations in the United States. Fast-forward to present day, and with my past endeavors and current management consulting business, The Thrival Company (www.thrivalcompany.com), I've had the joy and privilege of working in this field for 20+ years, in more than 50 different business sectors, all levels of federal, state, and local governments, the US military, and world changing non-profit organizations.

I have also been blessed to have studied under fascinating teachers, partnered with extraordinary change leaders, and built an incredible team of faculty resources. I was able to use my engineering brain to take fuzzy and amorphous principles of human behavior and craft them into clear practices that anyone can take on, use daily, and apply toward success.

The journey to cull years of data to create this book is something I now view as a fun, crazy, and enlightening 20-year research project. No matter how insane, frustrating, or impossible a project seemed, I discovered how much I love people in all their cultures, lifestyles, and views, and how at our core, we are similar in the ways that can allow us to make big ideas successful.

This journey has made the world a spectacular place to work and play in, no matter what circumstances were thrown at me. That level of excitement, passion, and energy is there for you, too. There is so much opportunity for you to be a success in taking that idea, that *Mission to Million$*.

What is the framework you will be learning?

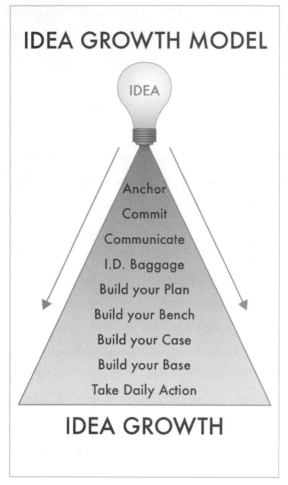

Each practice has been nested into a powerful 8-Practice Framework that will become your **Idea Growth Model**. The practices you will learn to master include:

- Anchoing your idea in reality.

- Utilizing the power of commitment to move forward and sustain performance.

- Communicating your idea effectively to others so they 'get it.'

- Identifying your 'baggage' that can cause your idea to fail.

- Building a plan to hold yourself (and others) accountable.

- Building your bench so you have the support you need to succeed.

- Building your case to inspire people into action.

- Building your base and creating a swell of support to make the idea a reality.

"Ordinary things done consistently produce extraordinary results."

- Keith Cunningham

We will also address the resistance you'll naturally have to keeping on track by teaching you a practice to ensure that you take daily action. This new framework will replace the **Idea Stagnation Model** (discussed in Practice 1) most of us have learned from our childhood and that has been reinforced throughout our lives by cultural norms. We will discuss that model in detail in Practice 1: Anchor.

Following this growth model for ideas, big and small, will ensure a shift in your abilities to succeed in making your great ideas happen. *"Ordinary things done consistently produce extraordinary results."* Keith Cunningham.

My gift to you is my ability to take ideas, and empower people to create them in the world. What is your great idea(s)? Let's get it done now . . .

ANCHOR

*"First comes thought;
then organization of that thought
into ideas and plans; then
transformation of those plans into
reality. The beginning, as you will
observe, is in your imagination."*

- Napoleon Hill

Practice 1 involves remembering and reconnecting with your imaginative self and getting those big, hairy, audacious ideas out of your head and visible. To do this, and not lose ideas over time and circumstance, means you have to take your ideas and anchor them in reality.

Anchoring an idea is important, because most of our ideas die before they see the light of day. In other words, they never make it out of our minds and into our speaking or writing. In many ways, ideas initially come to us like a love affair. The first phase is glorious, passionate, exciting and scary, and it comes with strong emotions. I am referring to this phase as The Love Affair of idea generation.

As is often the case with love affairs, the passion eventually fades as the reality of the situation sets in. Enthusiasm and focus become blurry, and you start losing sight of why you got into the affair (i.e., decided to commit to the idea) in the first place. You have settled into the Blurry Vision phase of your idea. More time goes on, and you remember why you had this idea you really loved, but it feels like it will take a lot of work to make it happen. Then, you hit dead ends and you don't know where to go with it. You feel like you're swinging blindly in efforts to make it work. You have reached the Blind Vision phase. Finally, you completely lose focus and commitment and you hit "idea death".

Before you begin to feel depressed, the best news about everything I'm relating to you is that the first step to success, anchoring your idea, is not hard. It's not rocket science (although you can make it seem like rocket science is required to do it). In fact, anyone can rally a community to deliver on an idea. This means you can stop waiting for the right person or circumstance to show up to make your ideas happen.

Reconnecting you to your imagination

Do you remember the first time you had an inspirational or aspirational idea? How old were you? Do you remember the rush of energy, the excitement? Did it seem like every worry, every muscle ache, and your fatigue melted away in that moment? You were *in the flow*. It felt fantastic. At that moment, it was the best idea in the world to you, and you couldn't wait to see it come to fruition.

Then, for many of you, you shared it with your mom or dad, or someone you loved and admired, and WOW…their 'no' or 'not possible' response felt like cold water in your face—shocking! You may have persisted and tried another route and hit another roadblock. Maybe you tried a few more times, but after that, the idea floated away, and you returned to the status quo and accepted that things were not going to change. You may have even felt like a tiny bit of your spirit died.

That's a great idea in theory Johnny but in the real world...blah blah blah blah...

If this pattern has continued through to your adulthood, you may not be where you want with many of your big ideas. You may have gotten used to your circumstances and told yourself it's okay that things didn't go the way you planned. You may still be looking for some spark of hope, or are feeling desperate and want to cry out for help even though your tough exterior is telling the world you're "fine." When a lot of your big ideas never happen, you may be feeling like you're barely surviving.

A *survival mentality* can be defined in many ways in our society, some of which are definitely positive and keep us physically alive and mentally stable in challenging circumstances. A good example of this would be the will to survive exhibited by prisoners of war who endured horrible circumstances and came out alive.

So, I want to be clear that for this book and the purposes of illustrating this discussion, I am defining a survival mentality very specifically. In the meaning I am using, this mentality is negative, because it limits our abilities to create and anchor our ideas.

SURVIVAL=DECISIONS BASED ON FEAR AND SELF-PRESERVATION

THRIVAL = DECISIONS BASED ON POSSIBILITY AND GROWTH

Therefore, I don't believe in a survival mentality in the idea realm, because merely seeking survival sucks the energy out of you. It sucks the creative energy from your personal life. It sucks the creative energy from

People who stay in an unhealthy survival state of mind find it difficult to create great ideas, and often make poor business and life decisions.

your professional life. It leaves you drained. Survival mentality can even make you physically and mentally sick.

People who stay in an unhealthy survival state of mind find it difficult to create great ideas, and often make poor business and life decisions.

One powerful way to move you out of survival mentality is to master Practice 1, which helps you re-connect to your imagination and re-energize your creative mind. Practice 1 is energetic training to support you in capturing big ideas that may have lain fallow, untilled, and unsown because you had no consistent outlet for them to grow.

The bad habits we have been taught

The reason why most of our ideas fail and/or never happen is because we have bad habits around capturing and taking action on our ideas. It actually isn't our fault that we have these bad habits. This model is so inherent in most cultures, we learn it from a young age. So most of us, on the average day, follow what I refer to as the Idea Stagnation Model.

The average idea that comes into your head can, at warp speed, go through the Idea Stagnation Model and die before you even realize it. It might feel something like the following description, if you think about the last idea you had that didn't happen.

You have an idea, and you feel excited. Then, you mentally make note of it, and if it's a really good idea, you indulge yourself and fantasize about how great it could be if it happened. A certain percentage of you even make it far enough to take token action to test the waters and see if the idea might be able to happen. But, you rapidly get resistance, which can come from others, and often from within ourselves. Then, that familiar twinge of sadness or resignation sets in, and you quit pursuing the idea before you even get started.

As I have watched my own children grow up and become part of our cultural system, I am amazed at how quickly they learn to become resigned in the view that big ideas rarely happen, so they hesitate to pursue them. I have had to put a lot of effort into shifting this paradigm for them to counter the negative idea generation support they are receiving from their peer groups, some of their well-intentioned teachers, or even our friends and family members.

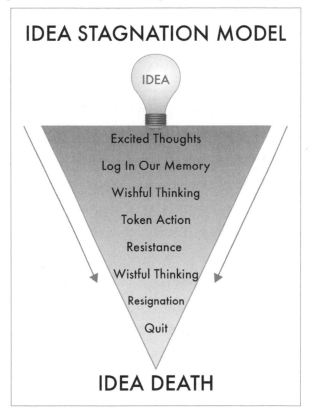

IDEA STAGNATION MODEL

IDEA

Excited Thoughts

Log In Our Memory

Wishful Thinking

Token Action

Resistance

Wistful Thinking

Resignation

Quit

IDEA DEATH

So how do we shift from the Idea Stagnation Model to the Idea Growth Model?

Close your eyes for a minute or two and think of the last time you were inspired about something. What was it? How did you feel when you thought about it, talked about it, worked on it? Energized? Excited? Optimistic? Hopeful? Passionate? Anchor that memory and feeling into your mind. Now write it down. Read it out loud to yourself. Did reading it energize you? What if you read that weekly for the rest of your life? You have just experienced how to capture the energy of your ideas and keep them going.

So, how does this experience relate to Practice 1: Anchor? The goal of this practice is to get all ideas out of your head and get them visible to your eyes. The practice itself is simple. All ideas are written down, big and small. So many of our great ideas never make it out of our heads. We kill them automatically before they even have a chance to see the light of day or the support of anyone else. This not only kills the idea, but it can slowly crush your spirit and drain your energy.

Most of us never write things down regarding our ideas. The practice is simple, but if it was easy, all of us would be doing it, right? In order to make it simple and build your mastery of the practice, here are some steps to follow to anchor all of your ideas.

AN ALTERNATE POSSIBILITY:

At an organizational or systems level, managers who don't recognize this critical process of encouraging their employees to generate ideas and anchor their ideas over time will fail to innovate, and run the risk of losing relevancy over time and in some cases, no longer be in business. Every person in every company should have a process they use to capture the ideas of their employees and vet them on a routine basis. If your current organization doesn't have an idea-anchoring process in place, get one implemented quickly. You are losing money and opportunity by the minute. The average person comes up with dozens of ideas daily that they either learn to implement or kill, based on your organization's culture.

Step 1: Create your Big Idea file

For step one, you will need to either have a physical journal, an electronic file on a PC, a notepad on your smartphone, or a voice recorder that someone can transcribe. The goal is to have your Big Idea file in a form that you can have with you at all times, save and add to it easily, and never lose it. For me, this is my notepad and voice recorder on my cell phone.

Step 2: Every time you have an idea, big or small, write it down

Take a pen or pencil, type, or use my favorite smartphone tool of voice to text and make a habit of writing down each idea you have as it occurs to you (or as soon as you can). Do not allow input from those little voices in your head telling you whether it's good or bad. (I know you have them. We all do.) Don't worry about punctuation or whether it makes sense. Just let it flow out of you like a river. There is no magic length, either. It can be one sentence or it can be pages. Just get it out of your mind and visible to your eyes.

Here are just a few short examples of some ideas that might come to you in the course of a day:

- **Idea 1 (Personal Idea)**: It would be really cool to do yoga twice a week.

- **Idea 2 (Big Vision Idea)**: I want to go into politics and be governor of Texas.

- **Idea 3 (Career Idea)**: I think I'm going to try to be the #1 sales person in my division.

- **Idea 4 (Social Idea)**: I wish my kid attended a green and healthy school.

Step 3: Schedule a weekly review of your ideas

Every week, take 15 minutes to review all the ideas you captured that week, and see which ones you want to move forward with. I love Sundays to complete this step, as we tend to be more creative and open on weekends (or whatever your days off are if you work a different schedule).

When you first get started doing this, you will be amazed at how many good ideas you've had over the course of a week. You will also see how many ideas you have *not* realized, because in the past you've had no process to capture them.

Step 4: Pick the ideas you want to make happen. Refine your language

Pick the ideas you want to make happen and write them powerfully. By powerfully, you should look for limiting-type words in the ideas you want to pursue, and take them out of the idea. The phrases 'try to,' 'hope to,' and 'want to' are psychological tricks that give us a get-out-of-jail-free card from making the idea happen. There is no trying, hoping, or wanting to make an idea happen. You work on it, or you don't. So from our idea examples provided in Step 3 above, here is a more powerful revision:

- **Revised Idea 1** (Personal): I do yoga two times per week.

- **Revised Idea 2** (Big Vision): I run for a political office by 2020.

- **Revised Idea 3** (Career): I am the #1 sales person in my division by December 2014.

- **Revised Idea 4** (Social): I become involved this year with and support organizations that advocate for green and healthy schools for my children.

Now read these ideas out loud. Do you see the shift in energy from the original idea? Now you have the foundation to move forward.

You can see that our ideas hold life energy. Each idea draws us forward out of survival mentality and into a thriving state of being. But, if you don't anchor the idea, it will fade quickly. You must master the practice of anchoring your ideas. Pull them out of your head and put the ideas in writing. Then, you can move forward into Practice 2 and make your ideas happen.

> **What about those ideas that are not quite commitments yet, but you don't want to lose them? Keep them on a second page of your Big Idea file. Review those tabled ideas quarterly, and see if any need to be added to your**

commitments. I have several dozen ideas that stayed on my list for a couple of years that I now have either made happen or am in the process of working on them. Sometimes ideas are not feasible at first but become more realistic with time, if you keep them in existence.

Steps to Success - Making Your Big Idea Happen Right Now!

Start capturing your ideas right now. Think about your career, your personal life, your community, and your dreams. Write them down. No editing permitted. For this practice, there are no bad ideas, only ideas. Capture every one of them. Put a reminder in your calendar to review them weekly. Build the habit, and you will master the practice.

SUCCESS STORIES FROM IDEA LEADERS

Luisa Mauro, Owner, Marathon Real Estate

Luisa Mauro's Italian family instilled in her the belief that owning property is the ultimate investment. She grew up with a true passion for the American dream. Memories of her

Sicilian grandparents growing produce on their own land, coupled with a keen eye for quality real estate, motivated Luisa to obtain her real estate license and become a broker. She has brought that family sense of investment pride to the real estate community, buying and selling rental properties, purchasing a commercial office building, and providing property management for her real estate holdings. She is also an avid runner, having completed 18 marathons, and has received so many awards recognizing her amazing performance, service, and community contribution they cover an entire wall. http://www.marathon-re.com/press

Q: Many people have to learn how to free up their minds to be creative, capture big ideas and make their big ideas happen. Yet, it seems to be part of your DNA to just 'go for it.' How did that happen?

A: I grew up in an entrepreneurial family, so that's what I've seen my entire life. My mom is British and my dad is Italian. On my mom's side, my grandfather had a clothing store in England. When we would go to visit him, we would see him working in his clothing store. My Italian grandfather was a farmer, but it was his own business, picking lemons, and he grew vegetables and fruits.

We moved to the States when I was four years old, and then my dad opened a business. That was the reason we moved to the States versus staying where we were or going back to England, like my mom had wanted to do. My dad said this is the country that gives us the most freedom, and allows us to open a business and have a chance at true success. It's so much harder in other countries.

So that is what I grew up seeing, and I was lucky in that I never knew anything else. I have never known what it's like to have to clock in at eight and be out by five. I have seen the long hours and I have seen that it offers less flexibility. What I do still has long hours, but it's worth it because it's your own. I wish I could say I had an 'aha' moment and thought, *oh, this is what I want to do,* but it's just been ingrained in me from day one to think about it and go do it.

Q: What gave you the idea for Marathon Real Estate?

A: Again, growing up, my Italian grandfather owned land. It wasn't worth anything at the time, but that is what he had. While I was in college here in the States, my dad decided he wanted to invest in real estate too. I was watching what he did and thought, *that makes a lot of sense.* Buy low, sell high; that's everyone's dream. What I really love about real estate is that while it's an investment, it's also a necessity; it's shelter. I really like being able to provide something that is a necessity for my clients, but also an investment, and being able to look at it both ways.

The reason we named our company Marathon Real Estate was because I have run eighteen marathons, and my business partner has run about the same. It goes back to my family and the way I was raised, and just being around real estate and believing that's the best kind of investment someone can make. I wanted to be able to take that and share it with friends and family, clients, and that's how it happened.

Q: How did you keep coming up with new ideas and take action? When I met you, you were doing more of the traditional residential real estate and now have you moved into larger investments and commercial properties.

A: What I found was, it was about consistency, and not just doing the same thing over and over, but improving upon it. You learn from every single experience, and while real estate in some form is consistent, there is always something unique and different that happens to everyone, so I am constantly learning. As for the action part of it, it goes back to the way I was raised. I was constantly told I could do anything I ever wanted to do, and to just do it.

Any idea I had or anything I wanted to do, my parents certainly supported me in it, so I have been really lucky with that. I also surround myself with people who support and believe in me. I have made a conscious decision to surround myself with really positive people, and it's a culture I try to keep in my business. I work really hard to keep everyone upbeat. Even my colleagues and my friends, if I look around, they're all people who believe in me, support me, and when I have a crazy idea, they'll do anything they can to help me.

Q: What are some of the things you do to move past obstacles, either within yourself or other people, to keep your idea moving forward?

A: It's the people I have in my life. I'm part of an entrepreneurial group, and I think it's important for anyone who wants to launch an idea like a business to find people who have done it already, and also those in the process of doing it. You'll be going through the same growing pains. I'm part of a group, and it's a subchapter

> **I have made a conscious decision to surround myself with really positive people, and it's a culture I try to keep in my business.**

of EO, which is Entrepreneurs Organization, and we meet a couple of times a month. We have a mentor in our group who has had hundreds of people in his companies and has sold them and done really well, and then the other people in our group have companies of similar size to mine. Some are larger, some are smaller, but they have gone through similar experiences. No matter how I may think no one else has ever gone through this, someone has. Hearing how they got through it and how they dealt with it, and having the support, is what helps me pioneer through it.

Q: How do you figure out who those people are that are going to be part of your support system? What are you looking for? What are your criteria?

No matter how I may think no one else has ever gone through this, someone has. Hearing how they got through it and how they dealt with it, and having the support, is what helps me pioneer through it.

A: Some of this happens naturally, like who we gravitate toward. Again, I'm very lucky. I have a very strong support system with family and friends. I think I have just naturally gravitated towards people who have an upbeat, positive attitude. The energy you can feel the first time you walk in can help you figure out if it's going to be a good fit for you or not. I can remember the first meeting of the group I'm in now. I didn't know if I ever wanted to go back, and it wasn't negative energy from the people. We were supposed to talk about the top three percent of what happens in our business life and personal life that we don't talk to anyone else about.

I'm a very private person, so going in and having to share and be open in front of five other people was very uncomfortable for me and very awkward, and I thought it went horribly. Thankfully I did go back, and it's a very confidential group. Nothing that is said in the room leaves the room. It was the energy I felt, and the support. I've tried other groups that didn't work, and the biggest thing for me was I didn't want a group where someone was paid to mentor me. I wanted to be in an organization where no one was paid and everyone is a volunteer, and we were going through the same things and wanting to support each other through it.

Q: If you met someone who had a big idea, what advice would you give them to help them make that happen?

A: Never give up. I think we look around us and we see very successful people and they make it look so easy, and it

Never give up. I think we look around us and we see very successful people and they make it look so easy, and it looks like it happened overnight. No one is an overnight success.

looks like it happened overnight. No one is an overnight success. I recently saw a quote from Adrian Brody, the actor, and he said "My dad told me, 'It takes fifteen years to be an overnight success,' and it took me seventeen and a half years." So that is the biggest thing I would tell people is to never give up and be discouraged because something isn't happening quickly enough. Often I think we stop and we give up, when we didn't know we were right around the corner from accomplishing something we really wanted.

COMMIT

"Unless commitment is made, there are only promises and hopes… but no plans."

- Peter Drucker

This book was intentionally set up as practices broken down into steps and actions to ensure you achieve mastery and move forward. If you read this book and never commit to completing each practice, your idea will stay just that—an idea. As Yoda instructed a young Luke Skywalker in becoming a Jedi Knight, "Do. Or do not. There is no try."

You have probably observed in life that there are 'talkers,' and there are 'doers.' Quite frankly, we all shift between those two archetypes on a daily basis. There are people who are going to start a business, and there are people who start a business. There are friends who are going to lose weight, and friends

> ## "Do. Or do not. There is no try."
> - Yoda from Star Wars

who lose weight. You can see the trend here. You are either doing something, or not doing something.

Therefore, there is no room for hoping, trying, wanting, waiting, attempting, thinking, (fill in the blank) if you want to turn an idea into a personal mission that delivers big outcomes. In Practice 2: Commit, you will be empowered to choose to make an idea happen or not. You will see firsthand the power of a commitment and how it can ensure that an idea happens. The proof is in the success stories of the people interviewed for this book. I refer to people who have mastered these practices as Idea Leaders. They are people you recognize every day in your family, workplace, and community, who seem to make big ideas happen consistently, sometimes over vast periods of time, and despite unfavorable circumstances that would seem to indicate a high likelihood of failure. Now it is time to master Practice 2: Commit.

We cannot direct the wind, but we can adjust the sails. (Ancient Proverb)

My breakthrough moment with the power of commitment came during my first performance review at my second job out of college. I got great reviews, 4 or 5 out of 5 scores in everything; except attendance at work. In that area, I was given a 1, indicating very poor performance. I was flabbergasted. I thought that I was excelling at my idea of becoming the best and highest-performing employee at the organization. I was working 50 to 60 hours per week and on the road constantly, taking

> **"We cannot direct the wind, but we can adjust the sails."**
> - Ancient Proverb

care of key clients. I was doing the job that I thought was being asked of me. But, I distinctly remember the manager telling me during the review, "The perception is that you just aren't here."

DEFINITIONS

Perceptions are a way of regarding, understanding, or interpreting something; a mental impression. Synonyms: impression, idea, conception, notion, thought, belief, judgment.

Views are a particular way of considering or regarding something; an attitude or opinion. Synonyms: opinion, notion, idea, conviction, attitude, feeling, sentiment, hypothesis, theory.

Congratulations, Elizabeth. We think you are amazing at everything you do... except show up at work.

It took me almost a year before I finally absorbed the wisdom of that review and took his comment to heart. Then I could distinguish the power of Practice 2: Commit. What I learned that day is that people's perceptions and views may not be fact, but they are the reality you and your idea are in. You must be awake and aware of these perceptions when working an idea forward.

When you have an idea, it is usually created out of a set of views or perceptions you have about something. For example, you have the idea, "I want to start my own business." You may have come to this idea because of a variety of views gained by what you perceive as your life experience, such as:

- My job stinks and the best boss would be to have no boss

- Having my own business would give me control over my life

- Having my own business will give me freedom to do what I want

- I can't get wealthy unless I own a business

- If I had my own business, it would be easier to make my ideas happen quickly

All of these views would give many people a very positive view of starting their own business. Yet, the facts mostly recently documented at the time of this book printing is that, according to Bloomberg, are that 8 out of 10 businesses fail in the first 18 months. According to the Small Business Administration, 5 out of 10 businesses fail in the first 12 months. These facts indicate that despite views of freedom and control, this 'start a business' idea can fail because it was launched under erroneous views on what are the realities of starting a business and having what it takes to succeed in business.

When I began researching the concept of how views and perceptions drive outcomes, I found that the action-specific perception model has roots in Gibson's (1979) ecological approach to perception.[1] In the simplest terms, people perceive their environment, and events within it, in terms of their ability to act.

Therefore, what I realized after that fateful performance review was that the basis for my idea of being the best performing employee was flawed because it was delivered via my own views and perceptions of how a person who is the best employee would act. When, in fact, the management valued presence, communication, and routine contact and reporting to demonstrate performance and presence.

Since my idea was driven by flawed views of what it took to be the best performing employee, I became very unhappy at that job, and felt resentful and unappreciated. That drove me to withdraw even further from the office environment, fueling the perception that I 'wasn't there.' As views shifted, so did my outcomes. My idea of being the best performing employee died.

I took this lesson forward to my consulting practice. When I talked with my clients, I always had to discern why they failed

---

1- Gibson, J. J. (1979). The ecological approach to visual perception.
(Boston: Houghton Mifflin)

or succeeded. It was, at the most fundamental level, due to an unconscious choice, just like I had made two decades before. They and I chose to use one of two performance models, and that unconscious choice drove their and my failures or successes.

The first performance model I refer to as the *Cycle of Self-Fulfilling Prophecy*. People who fail, quit, can't stay focused, waver, and over time stop trying to launch ideas do so because they're following a model of performance based on a set of perceptions and views. Those views drive their actions, and their actions drive their outcomes on that idea. Most of us have been taught to unconsciously follow this model from a very young age in most areas of our life.

The Cycle of Self-Fulfilling Prophecy

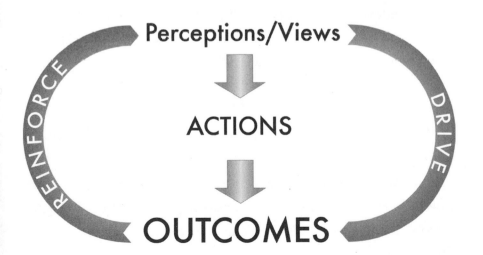

As you reflect on your own life, your perceptions and views are very transitory, and change over time. You may not think the same about something now that you did five years ago, or even an hour ago. So, if an idea is implemented using this model, as you get more negative feedback, you shift your views and perceptions. Then, your actions shift in response, and your outcomes become less successful. This reinforces more negativity, and you become more and more convinced based on your negative outcomes that you can't move an idea forward any longer from where you are.

So what is the model that Idea Leaders use to be successful and make their big ideas happen?

The second performance model is the *Cycle of Open Possibility*. Idea leaders use a subtle and powerful twist on the model presented above. Instead of using their ever-shifting views and perceptions to drive their outcomes, they make a commitment. In many cases, their commitment stands in the face of contradictory views, resistance, doubt, fear and failures. They are able to stand, and not waver in their commitment to their idea.

Commitment, in the context I use the term in this book, is not considered a rigid stance. It is in fact a very resilient, flexible, and open stance, which allows you to keep your idea moving forward even when the actions you must take to make it happen shift drastically. You stay committed to the idea even if your thoughts, feelings, or views change.

Commitment is the state or quality of being dedicated to a cause, idea, or activity, etc.

To illustrate the power of commitment, I am going to share a very personal story. In 2003, I was 100 pounds overweight after the birth of my first child. I had 'tried' to lose weight, and no luck. I was stressed out. My thyroid started failing. While this was happening, I was also working on a business start-up, launching a brand-new business venture in 2002. After a round of doctor's visits, my view of the situation was that my body was permanently broken, and the doctors gave me plenty of reasons to have that belief. Their words assured me that I would have these medical issues for the rest of my life. I believed there was nothing I could do to lose weight so I just pressed forward with the business, and gave up on my body.

One day, my then 15-month-old son ran off from me and headed into traffic. I was too fat and slow to catch him. I helplessly watched him go, and prayed the car would stop. Thankfully, it did. But that day, I went home grateful and

Commitment is the state or quality of being dedicated to a cause, idea, or activity, etc.

committed to the idea that somehow, and in some way, I would get in shape and be able to run faster than my son, because I never wanted to feel that helpless again.

I consciously chose to run my life under the second performance model—the Cycle of Open Possibility.

The Cycle of Open Possibility

Commitment

Your perceptions & views lose their power in the face of a commitment.
I am committed no matter what I think or feel.
I act in alignment with my commitments, NOT my views.

REINFORCE

DRIVES

OUTCOMES

I told everyone I ate with and spent time with socially that I was committed to losing weight so they could help hold me accountable. To be sure I did not shirk on my commitment, I took action on it. I took out a home equity loan to the tune of $11,000, as I was short on cash at the time, and hired a nutritionist-trainer for one year, as I had no idea how I could turn this around. I also took action to be sure I didn't quit by paying up-front for the entire amount, which was non-refundable, so I knew I would complete the whole time with her.

Whether I felt like it or not, she was at my house three days per week, and checked my food journal every day. Eighty pounds of weight loss later (which took me almost three years to achieve), I experienced the joy of racing with my son in ease and flow. In fact, I now had to intentionally let him win, because in my new body, I could fly past him.

That is the power of commitment. My views told me my body was broken, and I definitely perceived a painful, non-functioning body. But, I was committed to running faster than my son. This is an example of two different models of performance, with drastically different results.

You can create an idea, commit to it, and change your actions to align with your commitment. The views do not magically disappear; they just lose their power to drive your actions. That is the power of the Cycle of Open Possibility.

AN ALTERNATE POSSIBILITY:

Right now, in the modern workplace, we manage ourselves and others based on our views of us or them, instead of what we are committed to achieving as a team. Think about how different the workplace could be if we managed ourselves and each other by what we were committed to, and not by our opinions and views of each other. How different would your interactions be with people if you took action based on commitments versus views and perceptions? Just a thought to ponder—how would you rather be managed in the workplace: by what people think of you, or by what you are committed to accomplishing in your career?

You can spot an Idea Leader from a mile away. Idea Leaders are the people who are known not only for their achievements, but by their ability to follow through on their commitments. Idea Leaders hold themselves accountable. They act in the face of fear. They make their idea a reality. They don't waffle. They stand their ground and let others shift around them. This may sound or feel scary in our 'duck and cover your arse (CYA)' society, but I believe that playing it safe is the new risky.

> **"Freedom is not the ability of commitments, but the ability to choose—and commit myself to—what is best for me."**
> - Paulo Coelho, The Zahir

It may sound counterintuitive, but there is unimaginable freedom in making a commitment and keeping it. "Freedom is not the absence of commitments, but the ability to choose—and commit myself to—what is best for me." Paulo Coelho, *The Zahir*. In commitment, you can have all of the views, thoughts, feelings, and perceptions flow through you and be a part of you. They do not magically disappear. But with commitment, you don't have to be indecisive, let your doubts influence your actions, or defend your commitment. You just have to commit and then be willing to practice, practice, practice. So when I say *commit* to the idea, what does that look like as Practice 2: Commit? Let's get started.

Step 1: Capture one idea

You probably have thousands of ideas that you may want to see happen, and probably have captured quite a few in Practice 1 already. So if you haven't completed your Steps to Success from Practice 1, take five minutes to write down all the ideas that immediately come to mind that you would like to make happen. Don't overthink this. Just write down ideas. As mentioned in Practice 1, this will become your Big Idea file.

Step 2: Create your commitment statement

In Step 2, from this point forward you're going to keep a *Mission to Million$ Journal* that contains your commitments. To build this practice, you will pick one (1) of those ideas to work with initially (you can always add more). You will next write out your commitment based on the idea you want to see happen.

So, looking at what you wrote down in Practice 1, what is the commitment you have to make to ensure the idea happens? These commitment statements are intended to capture the Big

Ideas you want to make happen, and will be as diverse as you are yourself, in your interests, passions, hobbies, and pursuits.

- **Sample 1**: I am committed to making Big Ideas happen in a way that supports people worldwide in being successful.

- **Sample 2**: I am committed to being the top sales person in my division.

- **Sample 3**: I am committed to helping people with serious illnesses know what all of their options are for treatment.

- **Sample 4**: I am committed to finding my dream job.

- **Sample 5**: I am committed to raising $10,000 for my favorite charity.

- **Sample 6**: I am committed to being in the best shape of my life.

Step 3: Create five (5) goals you will achieve to deliver on that commitment

The purpose of capturing the five goals is to get to a place where you can start taking action. Actions, discussed in Step 4, will evolve daily, as ideas are fluid in nature, and have to be adapted as the wind shifts. If you are stuck on what goals to write around your ideas, sometimes it helps to think about the following areas:

- **Career/Co-workers** - What do I want to do in my career around this idea?

- **Financial** - Do I have any financial goals around the idea?

- **Education** - What education do I require to deliver on this idea?

- **Family/Friends** - How could I involve my friends and family in supporting me in this idea?

- **Creativity** - What do I want to create with this idea?

- **Attitude** - Who do I need to be to make this idea happen?

- **Physical** - What things do I need to do to support myself physically to deliver on this idea?

- **Fulfillment** - What do I want to get out of making this idea happen?

- **Public Service** - Who do I want to benefit philanthropically with this idea?

A useful way of making goals more powerful is to use the SMART mnemonic. SMART criteria are commonly attributed to Peter Drucker's management by objectives concept.[2] The first known use of the term occurs in the November 1981 issues of Management Review by George T. Doran.[3] The principle advantage of SMART goals is that they are easier to understand, to do, and then be reassured that they have been done. While there are plenty of variants (some of which we've included in parentheses), I use SMART to stand for:

- **S** - Specific

- **M** - Measurable

- **A** - Aspirational (and Action-oriented)

- **R** - Relevant (and Results-based)

- **T** - Time-bound (or Trackable)

The principal advantage of SMART goals is that they are easier to understand, to do, and then be reassured that they have been done.

---

2 - Bogue, Robert. "Use S.M.A.R.T. goals to launch management by objectives plan". TechRepublic. 20 November 2013.

3 - Doran, G. T. (1981). "There's a S.M.A.R.T. way to write management's goals and objectives". Management Review (AMA FORUM) 70 (11): 35–36.

SAMPLE 1 GOALS

I am committed to making Big Ideas happen that support people worldwide in being successful

- **Goal 1**: I publish a book called *Mission to Million$* by September 20, 2014 that empowers people to take their ideas and implement them.

- **Goal 2**: I use the book as a platform to reach and empower one million people or more to fulfill their ideas through the book.

- **Goal 3**: I further their leadership abilities by writing two more books by September 2016 that empower people to further master their abilities in Idea Leadership.

- **Goal 4**: I create a support network called The Thrival School that ensures that people who read the book have a place to come and be supported throughout the entire idea realization process.

- **Goal 5**: I create an author charity funding model by using my book to fund charitable causes I am passionate about.

SAMPLE 2

I am committed to helping people with serious illnesses know what their options are for treatment

- **Goal 1**: I build an online service that provides medical research for patients diagnosed with serious illnesses.

- **Goal 2**: I figure out a way to hire people who can provide affordable, high-quality research and data on the best medical treatments available worldwide to anyone seeking options in treating and curing their illnesses.

- **Goal 3**: I start the service in the US and then can grow worldwide, and I have 100 US customers by December 31, 2016.

- **Goal 4**: I figure out how to measure the fact that this service saves people's lives because we made them aware of treatments they would not otherwise know about.

- **Goal 5**: I empower patients all over the world to take charge of their medical care, creating a highly educated group of citizens who demand the best treatments, causing them to be more widely used and more cost effective.

Whether you write one sentence on your big commitment page or you fill the page with a dozen ideas and goals, the important part is that you write it down. If you do not write it down, you will not make the idea happen. If you have more than one idea you want to fulfill, you may have multiple pages/sections, each with a separate idea commitment and goals.

> "The discipline of writing something down is the first step toward making it happen."
> - Lee Iacocca

As you build your strength, you will be able to keep more and more ideas going at once. Right now, I have 144 Big Ideas I will make happen in my lifetime, so I have 144 commitments in my *Mission to Million$ Journal*. I review each commitment on a monthly basis. During this review I confirm priorities, review which ones I should be working on to make sure I'm taking action, and I decide if any that are waiting need to be put in motion.

BONUS IDEA: As a bonus to help keep your idea energy flowing, make it a point every week to share the idea you're working on with one new person. You will be amazed at the resources that show up just from sharing it with people, who then know people, who then can help you get where you want to go.

Feeling overwhelmed already?

Work your way through this book with one idea. If that's still too much to start with, then just use this practice for one month, doing nothing else from the book. On this practice alone you'll see your idea move, build confidence, and naturally evolve to take on the rest of the practices. Remember—growth is a journey. Making an idea happen is an evolutionary process.

 ## Steps to Success - Making Your Big Idea Happen Right Now!

Start your *Mission to Million$ Journal.* Take five short minutes to write one commitment statement on one Big Idea. Everyone has five minutes. Don't let the enormity of the idea stop you from taking five minutes of time right now to start you on your steps to success.

SUCCESS STORIES FROM IDEA LEADERS

Charles Dicks, COO, uRide

In 2011, uRide Founder and CEO Robert Dicks approached his twin brother, Charles, about his idea of starting a new cab company based in Austin, Texas. Robert and

Charles were those car-less college students who paid their tuition by driving the night shift for Yellow Cab Austin. Growing up with a twin brother taught Charles the value of teamwork early on. Together they and several partners took a huge and risky leap. They left their successful careers to create a completely new market and service to college students and their parents, with nothing more than an idea and a commitment to overcome any barriers to making it happen. It has been a roller coaster ride, and Robert and Charles epitomize Practice No. 2: Commit.

Q: We get to see uRide now in its finished and polished form, but how did the original idea come to you that led to the service we all recognize now as uRide?

A: It was an evolution. Robert, my brother and our CEO, was in the Air Force stationed in Germany, and I went to visit him for our 30th birthday, as we're twins. We went down to this cool coffee shop in Amsterdam, and we thought this idea would really work in Austin. That was the start of our entrepreneurial journey—we just wanted to start a business.

In the seven years since that initial idea, we started to evolve the idea by asking ourselves, "What do we know about?" When Robert and I were in college at the University of Texas, we had both worked as cab drivers for Yellow Cab. It was a cool college job, as you worked the 7:00 o'clock in the evening to 7:00 o'clock in the morning shift, and in between fares you could study while you were at work. We also got to meet a lot of cool people. That led Robert to notice that there wasn't an environmentally friendly cab option in Austin, Texas. So, Robert said, "I'm going to start a company called Austin Green Cab Company and it's going to use environmentally friendly vehicles and focus on customer service."

> **We talked every night, bouncing ideas around.**

He did a lot of leg work in trying to work with the city council. Robert had many challenging conversations with the city about getting permitted as a cab company. They said, "It's a great idea, and we aren't going to permit you." He was hitting his head against a wall there, but there's a line in the city code that says if you're a driving service that is in the employ or in contract with a state organization, then you don't have to get the permits that cab services use. So he had an a-ha moment where he said, "Who needs transportation? Students. What is a state organization? Universities."

We talked every night, bouncing ideas around. We thought about just focusing on college students. It takes a lot of time and money bringing cars to college, and the car just sits there most of the time. That's when a lot of those pieces started to come together. We had a market we could focus on, which was students, and it was a huge market. We started looking at the market and noticing there are a whole lot of colleges out there, and a lot of students, and a lot of parents with the same transportation decision. And it happens every single year, and with a new crop every single year. All of those dots just connected and we said, "Let's do this!" That's how the idea was born.

Q: What were some of the thoughts that you told yourself, or others told you, that came up that could have killed this idea at any point?

A: In dealing with the City of Austin, we said this is impossible, it's too big. This makes so much sense on the surface, but then we hit the political realities of the original idea. We thought, this makes so much sense, we can just go tell the city and go tell the university and everyone is going to say that's an awesome idea, where do I sign up? That's not quite how it played out. In offline conversations, everybody says yes, but when it comes time to actually sign on the dotted line or formally offer support, that becomes much more challenging.

Robert did all of this legwork in working with the city, and had door after door closed on the idea because of the

Instead of focusing on the forty-nine no's, it's focusing on the one yes, then running with it and setting up a meeting and learning from each one, and not just shoving the idea down someone's throat.

system in place. The university was saying, great idea, but you want us to put our name on it to give you credibility. So we got stuck in that chicken-and-egg scenario, and we were there for quite a while.

Q: How did you get a breakthrough in that? That's a big hurdle to overcome.

A: It was Robert's efforts inside the university and absolute persistence, and finding the right connections and telling the story over and over. People started to connect him with other right people. Robert speaks often about just putting it out into the universe and pushing, and then listening, and the right connections will come to you. He just kept putting it out there. Instead of focusing on the forty-nine no's, it's focusing on the one yes, then running with it and setting up a meeting and learning from each one, and not just shoving the idea down someone's throat. Put it out there and listen to the people's feedback and adjust the message, adjust the plan. Let the universe do a lot of the work.

Q: So you had removed barriers and were ready to go. Then what happened?

A: Robert had been nurturing another relationship with an older gentleman who had contacts to money. So we said okay, we were all going to leave our paying jobs within a six-month period, as we thought we had a lock on the investment and the money would be coming through in November of 2013. I resigned from my job in September and said, "I'm going to live off my savings." It's not like I had piles of gold, but I was going to adjust, and I had enough to eat. That was also around the time Airbnb came across my radar, so I rented my home, and that was enough to cover my mortgage.

For a number of reasons, that investment didn't come through. That was a big blow because we had a lot of plans and we built a lot. In our particular model, unlike cabs, or Uber or Lyft (companies people often compare us to), we're the most capital intensive. We hire our drivers, we spend money in training our drivers, we purchase our vehicles, and we need to market our services more because it's a new thing. It was like a punch in the gut. So we had to do a lot of soul-searching, and we decided we were going to make this work.

Robert, my Chief Technology Officer (CTO) and I just started digging into our retirement savings and self-funding the company. In the meantime, we were able to get some angel investors, some friends and family, $15K here and $15K there, people who believed in the idea and couldn't raise a lot, but could give us a lifeline. That has allowed us to get where we are right now, which is getting ready to close on our initial seed investment amount through Angel Networks.

Q: What was one of the hardest lessons learned in this process?

A: One of the things none of us realized is how much time fundraising took. It would consume sixty to seventy percent of our days, when we also needed to be marketing and growing the business. We didn't know how much effort and how many conversations and how many questions were going to be asked and how many documents there were to fill out. We had no idea what an effort it was to raise eight hundred thousand dollars. That's a whole lot of money, and it's not coming from a bank, it's coming from people's wallets, so that's a big sell. They have to be very, very comfortable with you and with the idea.

Q: You started touching on the marketing side of it. So when you came up with the idea, how did you come up with the right message to get parents and students and the universities talking to you?

A: It came to us pretty early on that we had a bit of a marketing challenge, and that the users in a lot of cases were going to be different than the payers. We identified early on that our true customers were the parents, and what we were truly selling was peace of mind to parents.

Q: How did you get to that messaging?

A: It was a lot of conversations internally and with students and with parents. I really can't nail down that it was that one a-ha. Really, it's just going through those conversations about what problem are you actually solving. Originally that was one of the things we were trying to position ourselves or market ourselves as, was a safe ride home. What we're really trying to do now is be an alternative to private car ownership. Who pays for the solution that's in place right now? The parents. They're the ones paying for the cars, so who are you going to have to convince not to buy a car, but rather purchase a transportation plan? The parents. It seems very obvious to me now, but in reality that messaging process probably took a year of internal discussions and talking with people we trusted.

Q: One of the other challenges when you have an idea is getting the right people to make it happen. How did you figure out who that was?

A: At least for the first couple of years it was really just Robert pounding the pavement, knocking on doors, networking and making connections. He would call me and we would bounce ideas off of each other. Then, Robert took the approach of telling as many people as possible, with no concern that someone could steal the idea, and see what connections were brought to him. That's a big challenge. Robert believes in the big world theory, and transportation is a big, big world. There's plenty of room for people to participate in it. If he didn't share this idea, then it was going to live and die inside him. He was absolutely right, because as much as he talked about it, that's how many connections came to him. He didn't go in with any special relationship with anyone inside the university or inside the city channels. It was simply using the resources we had and the connections we had and pushing it out there as much as possible, and letting them connect the dots in their own head and then making the right introductions.

Q: If you were to give the readers of this book any advice on how to make a Big Idea happen, what would that be?

A: Have lots of conversations and validate your idea. Let people punch holes in it, and make sure it's not just brilliant in your head. Once you have the conversations where people say, "I think this has legs," and you have done your research and there's actually an economic incentive for this, then you have to convince yourself this is a good idea. Then, eliminate all doubt. Take fear out of the equation, because this is the scariest thing I have ever done in my life. We have been on the verge of financial collapse more times than I can count.

Have lots of conversations and validate your idea. Let people punch holes in it, and make sure it's not just brilliant in your head.

Make sure you have enough faith in your idea that it will carry you through those extremely dark and scary times. There are times when you're going to have to put in more hours than you thought you had in you. Make sure, if you can, that you have a support system of your family and friends before you jump in, because they're going to have to support you through all of this.

COMMUNICATE

"The single biggest problem in communication is the illusion that it has taken place."

- George Bernard Shaw

The first time I walked into a board room, many years ago, was a remarkable education for me. I was helping a non-profit organization work on their strategic planning. The group had an inspiring idea, but was very low on volunteers and funding. In an attempt to build rapport with the board members, I asked them, "What is your vision for this organization?" What I received were uncomfortable stares and a lot of silence. Thinking that my question was poorly phrased, I rephrased my question and asked them, "In your own words, when you are talking to people about the work you do, what do you tell them?" That time I heard a few vague answers. Finally, feeling a bit frustrated, I asked them, "What do you tell your family about why you volunteer your time as a board member of this organization?" One board member laughed at the question and replied, "My family really resents all the time I spend on this non-profit, and they have no clue what I do here."

We have the best service in the world, but no one outside this room understands what the heck we do.

I knew there was a breakthrough behind his seemingly small joking reply...so I asked him if it was okay if we talked more about why his family felt this way, as it must make it really hard to do this work with no support of his family. The conversation went something like this:

"Why does your family resent what you do?" He answered, *"They don't understand the importance of it."*

"Why don't they understand how important it is?" He replied, *"Most people don't understand what we're doing because it's too technical, and I can't figure out how to explain it."*

"Why can't you explain what you do to your family in a way they understand?" He said, *"They aren't designers, and it's just too complex."*

"So, what do you think is the connection between your lack of supporters and funding, and your lack of support from your own family?" At that point he laughed and said, *"I guess neither one understands what we're doing, so no one wants to give us money for it."*

Now we were getting somewhere! This scene has repeated itself over and over again as I have worked with thousands of board members, company leaders, entrepreneurs, and professionals across the nation to help them understand why their great ideas and initiatives are not moving forward. My goal is to get them moving forward again and back on track to making their big ideas happen using Practice 3: Communicate.

The truth is, we often spend excessive amounts of time and energy working on the idea—building programs, and projects, and plans, and campaigns—while neglecting the mastery of communication about it. We often plow forward thinking like the movie *Field of Dreams* that "if we build it, they will come". As George Bernard Shaw so eloquently pointed out in the quote at the beginning of this chapter, we often labor under the illusion that we have communicated our ideas, but in fact we have failed to communicate them at all.

If you can't speak about your ideas clearly, you can't rally or sustain followers, donors, investors or even your own family behind you. When you are unclear on how to communicate the idea, resistance happens; not because it's a bad idea, but because they don't get it. Eventually, your poor communication can lead to failure. And that failure will push you back towards that old Cycle of Self-Fulfilling Prophecy by falsely proving to you that you tried, and the idea failed to happen, so you should quit.

Communication versus Vision and Mission Statements

Once you have anchored your idea within your own mind, the idea grows and gains momentum with how you talk about it in conversation with others. If you're working as an individual, you may write down a personal vision and mission statement. Large organizations may spend time building organizational vision and mission statements as well as charters around ideas. But, neither people nor organizations should communicate their ideas via vision and mission. With few exceptions, most people are not inspired to action by vision and mission statements.

In the past, when in an ornery mood, I was known to pull out a watch and ask a random organizational leader to tell me about the vision and mission of their organization in less than 60-seconds. Ironically, most of them would be stressed because they thought, "How can I possibly tell her everything she needs to know about our vision in 60-seconds?" What they typically found out was that 60 seconds was an *eternity* when you don't know what to say or how to say it.

The first place your idea will be borne is through the conversations you have with your family, friends, fellow leaders, managers, board members, co-workers, and community. I have seen some people knock it out of the ballpark in less than 30 seconds, and seasoned professionals who lead large organizations stutter their way through a very painful minute. Where do you think you are on that spectrum?

Neither people nor organizations should communicate their ideas via vision and mission. With few exceptions, most people are not inspired to action by vision and mission statements.

As the old saying goes, 'people in glass houses shouldn't throw stones,' so I can lump myself in failing for years to master Practice 3. I ran a business for five years and could not explain my company's vision to a potential new client in 60 seconds.

That shifted for me when I became clear on the value of my ideas to them, shifting sharing the idea from my views and perceptions to understanding theirs.

If you think about *Men are from Mars and Woman are from Venus,* which introduced the now very famous male and female archetypes defined by John Gray…guess what? Then engineers are from Pluto, artists are from Saturn, politicians are from Uranus, and our family members herald from multiple, unknown galaxies. Yet, in order to create a big, world idea, you have to speak it in a way that your entire target audience gets it. So, how do you do it?

The reason I struggled to verbalize my ideas in the beginning was that I was trained to 'sell' my ideas using a very traditional model of sales, which looked something like:

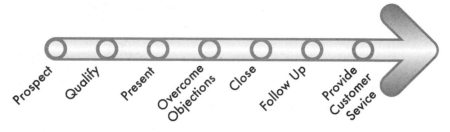

But to be effective at making ideas happen, that traditional sales model falls short. The goal of sharing your idea is to show the value of what you are offering in *their* view, which in turn motivates the person with whom you are sharing to want to *do* something. You want to *cause* something to happen as a result of your conversation, making it a *causal conversation.*

So instead, your idea sales model looks more like:

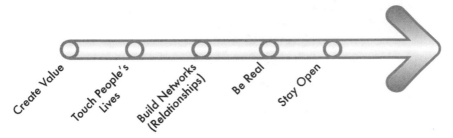

You start with the value your idea has. Then, you use that value to touch people's lives and engage them. This naturally leads to building a network based on the people who see the value. You continue to be authentic and be real as things progress, maintaining a high level of integrity. Then, you stay open throughout the entire idea creation process and be willing to shift your sails, adapt to changing circumstances, and keep encouraging feedback and building a deeper relationship with your networks.

How to create your One-Minute Mission Message (Your OM³)

When I was writing this book and attempting to come up with a title, I was working on this chapter. I landed on *Mission to Million$* because I felt that once you have an idea and are committed to it, it becomes your life mission to make that idea happen. If you can nail your idea and verbalize your mission's value in 60-seconds, I believe you are exponentially making progress to a successful outcome, and saving yourself more

The first step towards crafting your OM³ is to identify the value of your idea for the target audience, the action(s) you want them to take, and the outcome(s) you want to produce.

work in subsequent practices because your simple messaging will become *their* messaging The network will grow and build the brand of your idea for you. It is important to be aware that you will have multiple forms of your OM³ depending on your target audience.

The basic steps for crafting it concisely follow.

Step 1 - Identify the value, actions, and outcomes

The first step towards crafting your OM³ is to identify the value of your idea for the target audience, the action(s) you want them to take, and the outcome(s) you want to produce. You will have more than one variation of your OM³ depending on the person you are talking to. Your audience could be a potential donor, investor, partner, advocate or sponsor. The conversation could be at a social gathering with family and friends. You might be working with children in a school setting. You may need to get your co-workers on board. You may need to secure the support of a politician. You may just need someone to volunteer time to get something done.

You can identify the value for the person(s) you are speaking with by researching their views and perceptions around a particular idea. If you don't know them personally, you can do research online, talk to people who do know them, research their industry or area of expertise, and reach out to professional and social organizations they might be involved in.

Be clear on actions, as you want to leave them with some type of request to produce a desired outcome. Potential outcomes you may want to achieve include: get engagement, have them come to a meeting, prompt a donation or investment, enroll someone to work on the project, receive a referral, or just have them spread the message to other people or market your idea.

Step 2 - Figure out how to explain the idea in plain language

One of my favorite causes I personally donate time and treasure to is the *green building movement* led by the U.S. Green Building Council (USGBC). Some of you will think, "Cool." Others will think, "What the heck does that mean?" Another group will associate the *green* with money, and assume this has to do with finances.

You can see how one simple phrase, '*green building movement*' can be misinterpreted. You can guess what happens when you spew out a beautifully crafted statement using assumptions about people's understanding of terms to the general populace… 200 separate points of misinterpretation.

The truth is that many times, the vision statements we create around our ideas are only meaningful to those of us who create them, but may mean nothing to the general public or even to our potential 'fan base.' In the last five years, I have seen a large shift by both for-profit and non-profit corporations to create visions and mission statements that inspire people to join their idea instead of defining the organization's core values.

I still remember coming home one night and telling my husband how I was working with this exciting new client, the USGBC, whose vision was that "Buildings and communities will regenerate and sustain the health and vitality of all life in a generation." I loved this vision statement because, quite frankly, I would be what is defined as 'the choir' for the USGBC. This vision statement held meaning because it was preached in the language I understood. My husband's comment back to me was, "That's the worst vision statement I have ever read. What the hell does that mean?" My husband would fall into the category of the 'non-choir.' The vision was meaningless, and did not inspire him at all.

That night I sat down with their vision statement and thought about how it should look to someone outside of their organization. How could I break it down into language that could be understood by all? In reality, everyone was impacted by what the charity was doing. So what was going to be my OM^3 for their target audience?

By stepping into the non-choir views and perceptions, I was able to identify the value of their vision and also find a way to share the idea in a universal language that most people could comprehend.

Did you know that we spend 90% of our lives inside buildings? Home, school, work, play—all are in buildings. Yet, our buildings can destroy our health and environment when designed wrong. When designed right, they support our health and welfare and inspire us at work and play!

The U.S. Green Building Council's mission is not achieved through the green buildings it pursues, but rather through the people who live and work in them. USGBC trains and empowers you to get in action to advocate, educate, and transform your community so every person can live and work in a healthy environment.

When you work with us, you help your community by reducing poverty and homelessness, ensuring everyone can live in an affordable healthy home and build high-performing schools, which help your children learn better and protect your children's health.

Would you join us?

I have used this version in my own words, for all different types of audiences, and they get it. It still describes the vision, but in a way people can see, touch, and envision for themselves what this may mean in their own lives.

Step 3 - Script your One-minute mission moment (OM³)

Since I'm an engineer, my mind constantly learns things by breaking them into steps I can replicate. One of the things I noticed quickly when I first started sharing ideas and teaching others to share their ideas was that some were very successful, and others fell horribly flat. I realized that in those instances that did not go well, we had deviated from the value and outcomes we had identified.

Know the value, actions, and outcome you want to produce, and talk about your vision in plain language. Below is a script you can use for taking those key nuggets into a conversation that can produce the desired outcome. By learning to focus the communication of your ideas using this script, you can achieve the same positive results I experienced when I could finally communicate the USGBC's vision in language my target audience could understand.

OM³ Conversation Script

1. Connect with them

Many times we are so focused on getting what we want out of someone in our personal or professional lives, we forget we are talking to a human being with thoughts, feelings, and needs. This person may in fact be on guard because of their position or circumstances. It may not be a good time to talk to them. A genuine and heartfelt interest in them, their day, and checking in to see how they are doing makes a big difference for most people. Focus on the connection and relationship you want to build with them.

2. Share your idea simply. What is the value to them?

What is going on with you? What is your idea? Give them a short context for why you are having the conversation. You should be able to share your idea in less than 30 seconds.

3. Give the reasons why action is needed

✓ What is happening right now?

✓ What will happen if no action is taken?

✓ What could happen if your request is followed?

✔ Who will benefit from their support?
(possible charitable slant)

4. Make the request of them

So many times we don't get what we want from a conversation because we don't clearly ask for what we want. We are TERRIFIED to come out and ask. We will ask vaguely, we will ask mumbling, or we will ask like we are expecting a "no." I can't say how many times I have watched people skip or gloss over Step 4. I have even witnessed people state "This is probably a no for you but…" Take the time to write down what you clearly want. Then ask in a way that gives them an option to say "Yes," "No," "Maybe," or gets their opinion of a better possibility than what you have asked or proposed.

5. Complete the conversation

✔ **Yes** - Okay, what are the next steps?

✔ **No** - I would love your input on why, or would you be willing to do 'x' instead? Who else should I talk to?

✔ **Maybe** - What do I need to provide that would make it a yes? Or do I need to get you more information to help you decide?

✓ **Expertise** - Everyone knows something that might help you fulfill your idea. Invite them to share with you what they see is possible and where you should go next no matter what their answer is.

6. **Always acknowledge and thank the person sincerely and heartfelt, no matter what response you receive. They just gave you their life energy (time) to listen to your idea.**

Don't forget that your focus in communicating your idea should always remain on the receiver, and the value you give them by engaging with you. This applies whether you're an individual approaching a person directly, or whether you're working on an idea for or with a for-profit, non-profit, or government agency. The delivery of the idea (whether it be a product or service) will look different, but at the end of the day, people will stand with you because you're providing them something they value personally and/or organizationally.

What are phrases to banish from your vocabulary when sharing your idea?

I am requesting that you banish certain phrases from your idea vocabulary. If you are committed to your idea happening, there is no room for "try to," "want to," "hope to," "need to," or "thinking about" when it comes to achieving the idea. You're either committing to it, or not. If you use these indecisive phrases in your OM³ conversations, you can drastically change your outcomes to the negative side. Feel the impact of *try to* in a simple sentence:

- **WEAK:** At The Thrival Company we **try to teach** people how to make big ideas happen consistently.

  We hope to reach 1,000 organizations in the next year.

- **POWERFUL:** At The Thrival Company we **teach** people how to make big ideas happen consistently.

  We will reach 1,000 organizations in the next year.

Which organization would you rather hire? The one that is committed to their goals, or the one that is trying and hoping they might get there?

Feeling resistance to scripting? If you feel resistance to crafting anything in advance because it feels like it reduces spontaneity or will sound rehearsed, fear not. When you put your passion and commitment for the idea behind your conversation—and I'm assuming you have a commitment to you the idea you're sharing—nothing about it will seem rehearsed. The rehearsal and scripting that I'm asking you to do will give you the comfort to express yourself anywhere, and the clarity to explain your idea to anyone.

 ## Steps to Success - Making Your Big Idea Happen Right Now!

Take 15 minutes of time to craft and practice your first OM[3] around the idea of your choosing. Sometimes it's fun to just learn how to use the script on something simple, like convincing a spouse to go somewhere specific on a date night, or asking your friends to help you throw a party.

To gain comfort, you can practice first by yourself and record it (smart phones work great) and then listen to it. When you're feeling braver, share with someone (and if they're similar to your target audience all the better). Pick people initially who can give you feedback in a supportive fashion if you have issues with receiving criticism constructively before going out to a broader audience.

By mastering this practice, you'll be able to move faster through the early stages of making an idea happen. The person you'll be sharing the idea with will appreciate the time you spent to be clear. They'll also be clear on the value to them and your request of them, so they can make a decision.

The power of communicating the idea effectively cannot be over-emphasized. Share the idea and keep sharing it over and over again. Use your community and networks to keep your idea alive and point you to more and more resources to make your idea happen.

SUCCESS STORIES FROM IDEA LEADERS

Chekib Akrout, AMD Senior Vice President, Infrastructure and Engineering

Karen Davenport, AMD Director of Global Real Estate and Workplace Services

When it comes to making big ideas happen, we naturally assume that all ideas are ones that people will like and rally around once they understand the value. Yet, in the business world, many 'great' ideas have to happen because of changing business conditions, and can have negative implications for employees impacted by the idea.

Many articles that ran in 2012 spoke of the dismal future of the personal computer market. In 2006, Advanced Micro Devices (AMD) shares were as high as $41. By 2012,

AMD shares had fallen so low that they were trading below the $2 mark. At that point, the common belief was that they would soon be acquired or forced into bankruptcy. Ultimately, AMD was faced with a choice—they had to completely reinvent themselves, or they were going to fail.

As part of their aggressive plan to Restructure, Accelerate, and Transform, they had to control their debt load. A cost-savings idea was proposed to completely restructure the real estate portfolio at their Austin headquarters, which would allow them to free up more than $150MM. The catch was that the entire campus would have to be re-designed, employee workspaces drastically changed, a new way of working would have to be adopted, and the entire workforce consolidated into fewer buildings and smaller, more open cubes. In less than nine months they made this idea happen, despite massive resistance. This project and other steps taken by leadership have made AMD one of the turnaround stories of 2014. Mr. Akrout oversaw the implementation of the restructuring of the campus from the executive level, and Ms. Davenport directed the efforts at the operational level.

Q: Coming from your positions as SVP of Infrastructure and Engineering, and Director of Global Real Estate, you had to work an idea through thousands of employees very quickly in

Be ready to answer tough questions, because as good as the big idea will seem in your head, it will always have some problems or challenges. If you're not ready to answer some of them, you'll lose credibility and get blocked immediately.

an area that people are passionate about and have a strong identity associated with—their office. You had to make an unpopular idea happen in a very short time frame. What advice would you give people who are responsible for communicating an idea that may not be well received?

A: Mr. Akrout: I would figure out how to translate that idea into a language that helps them appreciate and understand it. You can describe a big idea and people can see it as "This is a great idea," but unless they internalize it and it becomes something they can really understand from their perspective, then it's not going to go anywhere. Try to think about how that big idea will look, and how it will come across. Be ready to answer tough questions, because as good as the big idea will seem in your head, it will always have some problems or challenges. If you're not ready to answer some of them, you'll lose credibility and get blocked immediately. The resistance is so big you won't be able to take off like a plane. If you think about a plane, without understanding of the idea, you're not going to be able take off. You need to be able to generate that lift for your idea. You must anticipate the questions and the challenges you're going to face.

A: Ms. Davenport: I would say do not resist; be open, even if you think it's going to take you off track. What I learned was that in the past, I thought the logic and the merit of my idea should be first, and then try to convince people that this was the right thing to do. What I found out in this process, what worked best, was to sit back and listen. Listen openly and to everyone, no matter how ridiculous their point of view seems. If you take the time, they will then be open to listening to you.

I've found that if you've done your research and your idea has merit, and if it has logic, they will at least listen to it. I work with a lot of engineers, and if it can meet the 'engineer's test,' they will consider it. We had a very aggressive schedule, but taking that time up front to listen I believe was the key to moving forward quickly.

Q: You had less than a year to implement this huge idea. What are some of the lessons learned when moving the idea forward?

A: Ms. Davenport: Tailor your message to your audience. Knowing your audience is important. This idea was a top-down, no question, force function, financial impact, hence the aggressive deadline, which people can understand. Our executives wanted a sound bite about what 'it' was, so they gravitated to 'one size fits all,' which is an anathema to space management. We understood it could be presented as one size fits all at the executive level, but that's not what you want to do at operational levels. I would say influence the executives first, to be comfortable that the overall concept is simple, but when you're talking to the people who have to live with it, that is not the message. There will be adaptations at that level. At the operational level, one size fits all doesn't work, as it takes away all their motivation and all their individuality.

Q: What kinds of resistance did you encounter that blocked or slowed the idea down from going forward?

A: Mr. Akrout: Many things happened. First of all, the environment we were in was a time when the company was going down, and we were shrinking and taking people out. We were asking more and more of our people. So, we needed people to work harder to save the company and then saying, by the way, the bonus is gone because the company doesn't have the revenue. Then, we came to them and said we think the office space is too big, and we're going to shrink it. When it came to shrinking space, many people thought it wouldn't be workable. You get to a point where you're asking your people to do too many things, and then this last ask we made, we

We were able to form a core team of thought leaders, some of whom were our most ardent opposition, but they had a point of view and they were passionate. These people can be turned into your advocates.

were perceived as literally inhibiting them from making progress. That's the kind of resistance we had. It wasn't the type of resistance because they wanted more luxury, but they started to think "you have become really crazy" because you're taking away their tools they perceived they needed to work.

Q: What do you feel was the best way to get your team members on board, knowing that some of them had opposing viewpoints? How did you get them to come to the table and really play at this?

A: Mr. Akrout: I think what really helped us get things moving forward was to identify a couple of key players who had a reputation of being the most difficult or the most respected, and get them to turn around. The rest of the people then saw that and said, "If they can get that guy, then I'm okay." There's always the easy one and the difficult one, but they are key players who are known by everybody. They may be pointed at and criticized, or people may say how smart they are, or how vicious they are, or how complicated they can be. But, if they see them turn around, then they're okay. I remember this one employee came in with a huge ledger describing how stupid this whole idea was and all the problems. We had a one-on-one discussion and I listened, and said here is the problem, and you can solve it this way. He came out of that discussion asking if he could help out and I said 'yes'. That's what turned him around.

A: Ms. Davenport: The best way build the team is for them to have a very distinct objective and top-down support. At the very top it was acknowledged as a key transformational project in both people impact and in the dollar sense, so people were put on a team that was going to be impactful. There was an invitation to the team from their boss' boss. We were able to form a core team of thought leaders, some of whom were our most ardent opposition, but they had a point of view and they were passionate. These people can be turned into your advocates.

If you can get thought leaders together on a team—even if initially they're in opposition—they'll make progress at a very rapid pace. As opposed to people who think like you, but don't have the push or passion.

If you can get thought leaders together on a team—even if initially they're in opposition—they'll make progress at a very rapid pace. As opposed to people who think like you, but don't have the push or passion.

If it's an idea they completely disagree with, you must sort all that out, and you must listen to them. I think the top-down approach and the listening was the key to this success. It wasn't incremental change, it was step function change that was needed immediately.

Q: So how did you communicate the idea in a way that moved through resistance to the project?

A: Mr. Akrout: The most important method was to explain why the idea is important and why this idea has to take place now. Emphasize the why before trying to explain how. If you start with the how, there was not a really good answer to the resistance. They'll tell you, "You took my tool away and I cannot do my job." We spent most of our time explaining, at least from the executive side, why we had to do it. By explaining the why, they get the sense that something needs to happen to solve that why. Then, the conversation becomes how am I going to solve it versus this is stupid and doesn't make sense.

Q: What methods did you use to communicate clearly and get engagement to be sure you brought an entire campus of thousands of people together very quickly to execute the plan?

A: Ms. Davenport: You have to manage all aspects of communication and be on it. We had the emails and the very rigid cadence for our project communications, and then we had this free-flowing exchanging of ideas in other formats.

One of the things that we did, because this was a completely new work area concept, is we created mock-ups of work stations and the options. We had a facilitator from The Thrival Company come in and orchestrate that. That created a very hands-on approach that every person—whether you're a VP, engineer, administrative staff, or a technician—could come in and look at the work station and get questions answered.

Another thing we did was we had written feedback from surveys before we launched the project. I think that was very effective in getting a familiarity with what was going to happen. From the feedback, we also created a cadence of meetings

Don't assume when you communicate an idea with someone, and even if they understand it, that they'll be able to take that idea and communicate it to someone else. It's a bit like the game of telephone. It becomes a different message than you think it will be.

where we communicated at the highest level what was going to happen. So we hit the top and the bottom with meetings. The middle management was more of a hands-on communication approach.

We used an internal communication forum we have at AMD called Connect, where anybody can say anything they want. That was really off-putting to me personally, as I couldn't imagine what was going to be said or how it was going to go, so it was a little bit scary. But, we hired expertise from The Thrival Company to manage that part of the communications, which is a newer way to communicate. I can't gauge exactly how it moved the needle, but we know that there was an outpouring of opinion, which I think was good and appreciated.

Q: What are some common communication mistakes leadership make that can sabotage an idea and keep things from moving forward smoothly?

A: Mr. Akrout: Don't assume when you communicate an idea with someone, and even if they understand it, that they'll be able to take that idea and communicate it to someone else. It's a bit like the game of telephone. It becomes a different message than you think it will be.

When we talked about our idea, I spent time explaining the 'why' to other senior vice presidents, and I assumed they would be explaining it down the chain. That was a mistake. They either didn't explain the 'why,' or they couldn't explain the 'why' properly. It was not intentional from their side. They just couldn't take the discussion of the 'why' we were having at the executive level and translate it to the sub-divisions of the organization. To close this gap, we went deeper into the organization with town hall meetings. We had the same level of discussion that I'd had with my peers with their own directors, managers and employees, making sure they understood it. And they had the opportunity to ask questions.

Q: If there was one thing you want readers of this book to know about making Big Ideas happen in a corporate environment, what would that be?

A: Ms. Davenport: One word—patience. It's not easy. If you have a really good idea, its time will come. It may not come at the company you're at today, and it may not come with the boss you have today, but you just keep at it. That's really tough. I'm old enough now to be really patient, so if it's not in your nature to be patient, develop it, because it will happen. Its time will come, and you don't know when that is going to be. You don't know from whom it's going to come. Teach yourself to look around and have a broader view and be in the know. Be in conversations with a myriad of people because you just don't know where the solution is going to come from.

You have to own the idea, good, bad, and ugly. Whether it blows up in your face or it's a wild success, it's yours. So when you embark on this, don't shy away from owning it.

Q: Are there any other things people leading Big Ideas should consider when launching the idea?

A: Mr. Akrout: Having a big idea like ours was definitely the right thing to do. It was the right timing, and the reason we were able to do it was because the environment was right. We had the sense of urgency to do something that probably would have been impossible five years ago. So, timing is important.

You have to think about two questions. How many big ideas can you do at the same time? Also, what is the level of compromise you will accept? These are tough questions to think about. Frankly, there is no simple answer to them. It's quite complicated. Sometimes you want to say, I'm not going to get my next big idea right away, so I can recover. But then you can sometimes use the momentum from an idea to get to the next big idea. The other question is, what compromises are you willing to make? In this project, we backed off of some requirements and we compromised on some things, but we didn't change any of the outcomes we needed to achieve. We would come up with an answer. Then, someone else would come up with a different answer, and although we didn't like it or it didn't make sense, we had to compromise on that. But, we didn't have to compromise on any of the real outcomes.

A: Ms. Davenport: I would say it has to be "your" idea, and own it. You have to own the idea, good, bad, and ugly. Whether it blows up in your face or it's a wild success, it's yours. So when you embark on this, don't shy away from owning it.

Q: How do you stay in high energy when ideas have to be implemented all the time?

A: Mr. Akrout: I look back and appreciate a successful outcome, and that gives you positive energy to move forward. That's what you have to feed yourself with. You feel like you're winning, so you continue winning. If you feel like a loser, you will lose, and you will feel bad. It's a cycle, so you have to stay positive and celebrate to keep having successes with your ideas.

IDENTIFY YOUR BAGGAGE

"Why are empirical questions about how the mind works so weighted down with... emotional baggage?"

- Steven Pinker

When it comes to the human condition, none of us gets to grow up without bias, or baggage. Things happen throughout our lives that cause us to develop views on thousands of topics. They shape our perception of life as we experience it. Most of the time, our baggage hides itself in what is called the *bias blind spot,* a phrase created by Emily Pronin, a social psychologist from Princeton University's Department of Psychology, with colleagues Daniel Lin and Lee Ross.[4]

To illustrate this concept, I would like you to close your eyes and try to remember your earliest memories of money. What were you thinking? What were you feeling? What opinions did you form about money as a result of those memories? Now, jump forward to your teen years and again, recall a memory that involved money, and what opinions you formed. Can you see you may have formed some views just on this one topic of money that possibly impact your actions and outcomes in the present day?

At the age of six, I remember clearly that money was very scarce, and my parents worked hard at exhausting jobs to earn it. My parents frequently argued about money. Dad controlled it, and Mom begged for it. Would you find it surprising that in my early adult life, I worked myself to exhaustion and worried constantly about running out of money? I also made sure I married a man who gave me 100 percent control of my money, as I wasn't going to ask anyone for permission to spend it, or let anyone control me. As you can see, the money baggage I got as a child followed me for the rest of my life *until* I consciously set my baggage, i.e., bias blind spots, aside.

The bad news is that the baggage you're unconsciously carrying will either help you soar like an eagle, or sink you like a stone when it comes to making your ideas happen.

---

4 - **Pronin & Kugler (2006)** *Valuing thoughts, ignoring behavior: The introspection illusion as a source of the bias blind spot.*

And, in your current unconscious biased state of mind, you have no power or control over it. Your baggage will drive you to actions and outcomes automatically, and without you realizing it's even happening. The good news is, this chapter is all about mastering a technique to constantly identify your baggage, as well as other people's baggage. You'll also take the power of those views away from them so they can't negatively control your outcomes.

How do you find your baggage?

One way to identify where baggage might be lurking is to notice when your actions are incongruent with the magnitude of the request someone is making of you. When I first starting working in non-profit, I was surprised by the fact that, although I had been successful in raising millions of dollars of revenue for the organizations I worked for (including my own) and had completed projects that saved my clients hundreds of millions of dollars, I seemed to have a mental block about raising money for charity.

In my professional job, I could walk into a client's office, present a proposal, and receive funding for a project, whether it was $1,000, $50,000, or $1 million dollars, and be comfortable doing it. But, when it came to asking my friends, family, or co-workers to fund my favorite charities, asking for even $50 seemed uncomfortable and wrong. It was so bad for me that for years, the Leukemia and Lymphoma Society would send me pre-made letters and envelopes to send to my friends and neighbors that requested donations with a target of raising $100. Every year, rather than sign a pre-made letter 10 times that came with already addressed envelopes, I would not send the letters, and instead write them a check for $100. So to avoid completing a very simple request, I was willing to part with $100. That was a big red flag that I had baggage, baggage, and more baggage in this area.

When I volunteered to donate time and function as the development director of a small non-profit, I realized that a breakthrough was in order. Nearly everyone I met as I got more deeply involved in charitable work, from the boards, to the executive level staff, to the volunteers, was completely uncomfortable asking for money. What was up with that?

Thankfully, I do behavior change and culture change for a living. So, the teacher became the student, and I decided to use the Cycles of Self-Fulfilling Prophecy and Open Possibility we discussed in previous chapters. I had to dig into my own head to figure out what was going on so I could get myself and others moving in the right direction. As you remember, the Cycle of Self-Fulfilling Prophecy can be deadly, because it can put you in a cycle of failure around your Big Ideas. The failure results because your views and perceptions are constantly shifting, and if you let them control you, they can cause you to take the wrong actions, and move your idea in the wrong direction.

The Cycle of Self-Fulfilling Prophecy

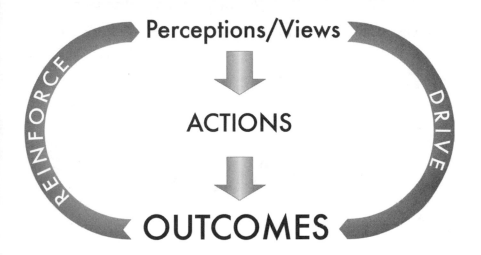

Another way to show this model is to state that in the absence of a commitment, perceptions and views drive actions, and actions drive outcomes. When I was failing to raise money for my favorite charities, the reasons for failing were buried in my views towards asking for money (one of which was that it was okay for me to give my money, but I had no right to expect others to give theirs to charity). Those views were unconsciously driving my actions towards that negative outcome of refusing to even ask for money. I was not a fundraiser, just a donor.

Once I was able to discern the views that were unconsciously preventing me from asking for money, I had a major breakthrough. In my current career evolution, I am now a great and fearless fundraiser. I teach courses on how to raise money for charities. Non-profits now hire me specifically to help them have breakthroughs in their fundraising abilities and results. That is a huge shift from the woman who wrote $100 checks to avoid even asking for money for a charity fifteen years ago.

Now it's your turn to master this practice. In order to succeed with your ideas, you have to become aware that you run your whole life based on a collection of views and perceptions that may or may not be true, which can cause bias blind spots in the way you think. Your view of money is just one of the pieces of baggage you have been carrying around your whole life. You have thousands of others. It's time to lighten your load. So how does this practice work?

When I shared about my own money baggage from my family, I realized I had a view that meant I had to work really hard to earn a lot of money. Money was very hard to earn from my past life experience. So my money baggage looked something like the graph below.

VIEW

**I have to work really hard
to get a lot of money.**

ACTIONS

**Work overtime.
Worry when I'm not working.
Constantly looking for more and more work.**

OUTCOMES

**Constantly overworked. Income based on hours.
Exhaustion. Stress. Degradation of health.
Disconnection from my family. Burn-out.**

I spiraled in the early part of my career in a never-ending cycle of stressful jobs, working overtime hours, and developing health issue after health issue until I identified this view. Because I didn't even know this view was driving me, I acted on it unconsciously, like it was true, until I realized it was just a view, not truth.

Now it's time to look at your own views and how they might stop you from asking for the support you need to make your idea happen. When it comes to your ideas, I have found that most people's idea baggage falls into seven distinct categories. You may have one of these pieces of baggage you're carrying around. Some of us carry all seven bags and more!

The 7 Views that Can Sink Your Ideas

1. The We're not Worthy View

If at the core of your being you actually don't think your idea is worthy, or more personally, *you're* worthy of investment, the matrix of voices in your head will feed your fears about this. *Who am I to do this? I don't deserve this. Who do I think I am? I'm not qualified. What if I fail? This is impossible. What if it doesn't work out? [fill in the blank] will make it fail…* We could go on and on about those voices in your head. Those same voices are stopping you from engaging with your partners, obtaining funding, and advancing your idea.

VIEW

I (We) don't deserve this.

ACTIONS

**Don't ask. Don't ask for enough.
Make 'token' asks. Ask half-heartedly.**

OUTCOMES

**No funding or little funding.
You prove your view that (we) don't deserve it.**

Can you see how these little self-fulfilling prophecies that you created in your head have absolute power over your actions? Let's shift your awareness by exploring a few more common views so they're no longer unconscious baggage.

2. The Honest Abe View

In this view, money, trust, and reputation has to be earned. I believe that I or my idea hasn't earned the right to be given these things. If you wait to share or take an action on your idea, or wait to ask for funding until you believe you have earned it, you may never make your idea happen. The whole concept of an idea is that it does not yet exist in reality. It might be a big, hairy, audacious goal (BHAG) to create a better world, better product, better service, or better organization. There may be nothing in the past that says it will work. It may look infeasible and feel unreasonable. People are going to question it. There will be resistance to the idea, even from those you trust the most, as the nature of culture is to resist change. The idea may so phantasmagorical that there is no way to even 'earn' anything

VIEW

Money, trust, reputation has to be earned.

ACTIONS

**You keep trying to perfect things.
No or minimal sharing/asking. You are not quite ready yet, so you
wait. Wait. Wait. Wait.**

OUTCOMES

Slow or no progression of idea, support, and funding.

concrete that would make you comfortable ever sharing or going forward with the idea. So let's show the impact of you working your idea from this particular point of view.

Now, having illustrated that negative outcome, I have one small caveat. You don't need to be perfect, but you *do* need a plan (Practice 5 in this book). Good planning is a practice you'll master, as it's a basic requirement of making your ideas happen consistently.

3. The Psychic View

In this view, we magically assume we know whether or not a person or organization has the money, time, or talent to give us. It's in our very human nature to pre-judge a person or an organization's ability to give you time, money, support, or other resources. And we will ask or not ask for what we need for our idea based on that pre-judgment by us or others of their ability to give.

Yet despite this common view, I still remember the first time my husband shared in a casual conversation with a close friend about a new charity project he had an idea to start. The idea had stalled, because he needed $1,000 to get it going and renovate his first home. This friend wrote him a $1,000 check. He was not a person of wealth. He worked a modest state government job. He lived a simple life. From my view of him, I would never in a million years have expected that this friend would give that much money to my husband for his idea, nor would I have asked him to give that much.

VIEW

They don't have the money, time, or talent to give me.

ACTIONS

Don't ask. Ask for a little bit.
Only ask someone if you think they can give.

OUTCOMES

No funding or resources provided.
Little to no resources to accomplish the idea.

My husband went on to raise money from people like his friend successfully. At this book printing, more than 45 homes have been renovated thanks to his willingness to ask for support without – pre-judgments. The lesson to be learned and taken to heart is that you should never judge anyone's ability to give. Give them the freedom and the power to choose to give to you for your idea, whether it be time, resources, or money. Ask for what you need, and give them a way to be a part of it. Don't choose for others!

> **THOUGHTS TO PONDER:**
>
> I remember at one of the first fundraising courses I attended, they showed the statistic from one of the non-profit research studies that stated that about 30% of us have surplus income to donate, yet 70% of us donate. What does that statistic mean? It means if people want to see an idea happen, they will not just give of their excess, they will also give up something they care about to fund a great idea.

4. The Looking Good View

Looking good is a big thing for almost every human being who lives and breathes, with few exceptions. (Even those who say they don't care about how they look take pride in their image of not caring how they look.) In this view, you're limited by your fear that you'll look bad, stupid, [fill in the blank]. It's little surprise that the Number 4 reason you won't share your idea or ask for something you need for your idea is that you don't want to look bad. That voice in your head has probably already started chattering again as I mention this.

What if I sound stupid? What if they think it's a bad idea? What if they think less of me because I asked them for money? What if they tell other people I'm a fool or what I'm doing? What if they tell me it's a bad idea?

By letting go of this particular baggage, there is a freedom and peace you'll reach. You'll realize that moment you choose to launch an idea—playing it safe will become the new risky. Just take a moment to watch the news. The people you see out there who are making change are swinging for the fences, sticking their necks out and having conversations for change. Will some people

VIEW

I will look (bad, stupid, _____).

ACTIONS

Don't as. Or, wait to ask until you have it perfect.

OUTCOMES

Paralysis. No or slow progression, support, funding.

criticize you? Yes. Will it hurt? It definitely can. Is that a reason to not ask? Absolutely not. This is where I tell you to go back to your commitment statements you wrote and learned about under Practice 2. Remember why you committed to the idea and why you're doing this. It's bigger than you, your identity, and your personal fulfillment. Don't let your ego take you out of the game.

You won't look back after succeeding with your Big Idea and say, "I wish I hadn't done this because I looked stupid while asking [fill in the blank] to support this project."

5. The No is Bad View

Our Number 5 view can stop you cold in your tracks when making an idea happen. In this view, when we hear no, that means something bad. Right now, you need to check in with your gut and connect with your emotions to realize how you feel and react when people tell you no. What is your view of no? What thoughts come into your head? I have helped guide people embarking on big initiatives through this exercise many times, and here are some of the most common views people take on when someone tells them no:

• I failed

• I stink

• I did something wrong

- They don't like me

- They don't like my idea or project

- There is something wrong with how I asked

- There is something wrong with the idea

- They think I am (or we are) incompetent

- They don't believe I (we) can do it

- I look like a fool

- Everyone else will tell me no, too

- Everyone else will think I'm a fool, too

You may notice that the first place you typically go after hearing no is to failure, and to focus on yourself. You can fail. The odds are in your favor that you'll fail in life, maybe once, maybe 100 times. We actually live on a learning planet, so failure is essential in order for us to learn as human beings. The difference between an Idea Leader and *everyone else* is their view of failure and their ability to let no just be no. Ask any leader you admire, and they will share stories of success and failure and what they learned. They're okay with failure. They're also okay with no. They don't make no mean anything that will stop them from keeping their idea in motion.

VIEW

**They will tell me no and
that means (I failed, I stink, _____)**

ACTIONS

Ask, but you stop asking at the first or second "no".

OUTCOMES

Idea/Visions Death

An alternate view of no

My mom used to joke to other people that I came out of the womb living by the slogan, "No is the start of negotiations." She was right. I have always viewed no as just the first step to getting a yes, and rarely internalize it as a failure on my part when I am told no. It's no surprise that my siblings had the view that I always got what I wanted from my parents growing up. Most of the time I did; but it was because I was never stopped by the no. In the fundraising world, the statistic varies slightly depending on which study you cite on how many negative responses you will get before a yes. On average, the success of a fundraiser in getting a yes when asking for funds trends with a really good batting average. That means 7 out of 10 times you'll miss the ball and you'll be told no. So, if you stop asking at your first no, your second no or even your third no, where will you be? Depressed, unsupported and unfunded.

If you instead adopt the view that every no is an opportunity, you'll learn and build lifetime relationships with people and be unstoppable. This alternate view of no has worked well for me in my career. I've built relationships with amazing people who have enriched my life, whether or not they enriched my pocketbook or supported my ideas. I was also able to find possibilities to make my Big Ideas happen in a way that was even better than I had imagined possible because I was told no by someone else.

An alternate response to someone telling you no

This is how your new view around no being an opportunity might play out in an ask situation around your idea:

- You share your idea

- They respond to your share and say no… SO WHAT'S NEXT?

- You say, "Thank you," and you appreciate their time. Say it helps you to understand the no so that you can be successful in launching this idea so would they be willing to give you feedback on why the no?...AND/OR

- You ask if you could get their input on the idea, what resonated with them and what didn't...AND/OR

- You ask who they think would be interested in this idea if not them...AND/OR

- You could ask if they'd like to receive information as the idea grows, so they can get to know you better...AND/OR

- You could ask them to volunteer time or expertise... AND/OR

- You could invite them to an event or program...AND/OR

- *THE LIST GOES ON AND ON ONCE YOU DROP THE BAGGAGE OF NO*

No is an opportunity to deepen relationships

Every no holds the possibility of building an even deeper and more fulfilling relationship with the person or organization delivering the no. Dr. Barry Morguelen, from the Morguelen

"The purpose of feedback, whether positive or negative, is to deepen your relationship with the person giving you the feedback."

- Dr. Barry Morguelen, M.D.

Energy Institute, which specializes in using energetic practices to drive success has been quoted stating, "The purpose of feedback, whether positive or negative, is to deepen your relationship with the person giving you the feedback."

By adopting his view of feedback, I feel energized and inspired, even when things don't go my way, simply from making an amazing connection with another human being. You can, too.

I recommend that the next time someone is giving you feedback, ask yourself, how can I use this opportunity to deepen my relationship with that person? Try on the view that everything they're saying will deepen the relationship. Notice how the outcomes of the conversation shift in that new perspective.

6. The Don't Bother Me View

In this view, we hesitate to share or ask for something around our idea because asking a person for something will make them uncomfortable. I often tell my clients it's not my job to make them comfortable. Change does not occur in comfort in our bodies. We work out, we get sore. The harder we work out, we always have that period of change or soreness in our bodies until it adjusts. This same principle applies around making new ideas happen. The most common place I see the Don't Bother Me view come up is when you have to ask someone for money. You don't want to make that person uncomfortable. In many situations, it's not okay in our society to openly talk about money, so we avoid that conversation.

VIEW

They will be uncomfortable with me if I ask them for money, time, or support.

ACTIONS

Don't ask frineds, family, co-workers, investors, donors, or anyone for help or support. Or, you sugarrcoat the message. Excessive worry about what they are thinking.

OUTCOMES

Stuttering. Justifying. Being unfocused and unclear with communication and request. Slow or no idea progression, support, and funding.

As money is a major reason people fight, marriages end, companies fail, and people's lives are enriched or broken, is it unreasonable, or any sort of surprise, that many people are uncomfortable asking for money? And from the potential giver's standpoint, being asked for money? I ask for, give, and invest money all the time, yet I still don't like being asked for money.

In some cases, I still don't like to ask for money or time, even after identifying my views on making myself and others uncomfortable. But, it's important to realize that being uncomfortable or making someone else uncomfortable is a necessary aspect of change and idea creation. It pushes you out of your comfort zone, and will probably push them out of their comfort zone also. All human progress is based on people committing to things that push society beyond where it is now, and that shift is uncomfortable. Acknowledge when you have this view, but don't give it power to control your asking or not asking.

Is being uncomfortable a show-stopper for you?

To give you some context on whether being uncomfortable is a show-stopper, here are a few questions to ponder. *Is there anything in your life that you do to improve yourself, attain a major goal, develop a new skill, be healthy, or start a new relationship that doesn't feel uncomfortable at some point in the process? Was it bad to feel uncomfortable? What would be possible if we never felt uncomfortable?*

Discomfort often causes us to create new possibilities, stretch ourselves, and grow our organizations. If there was no sense of discomfort, we'd all look like the morbidly obese characters who starred in the movie *Wall-E,* doing whatever it took to avoid making the slightest effort. Ideas are about changing the status quo, so get comfortable about experiencing discomfort, and realize you're offering the person you want to involve in your idea a possible future they may never have achieved on their own.

7. The Failure is not an Option View

In this view, it's not okay to fail nor waste anyone's time or money. It's wrong to fail. You're a bad person if you fail. Wasting people's time or money because you fail is bad.

Why is it so bad in our world view to waste money? Because money, at its deepest root, is an extension of our life energy. In the book *Your Money or Your Life,* by Vicki Robin and Joe Dominguez, I love their discussion about money. They state that because we only have a limited number of hours on the earth, and most people trade their time for money and their money for stuff, that means your money = your life energy. So when we ask for money (or even someone's time), we're taking a piece of their life energy. No wonder we get so stuck on having money conversations with other people!

Failure is another huge piece of baggage we carry around with us. We're taught it's not okay to fail. The famous quote that we've heard most of our lives is that "Failure is not an option." The reality is, failure is not only an option, but the faster you extract a learning from the failure, the closer you'll get to having success. The best Idea Leaders fail and go into learning and action quickly. It's important to realize that at the end of the day, some ideas will fail and sometimes fail repeatedly, even when you worked hard and did every step in this book to be successful. There are no guarantees when you take people's time, resources or funding that you'll succeed.

VIEW

It's not OK to fail. It's not OK to "waste" their time, talents, and / or money. It has to be a sure thing.

ACTIONS

No action. Token action. Timid requests. No requests. Only ask for a little bit. Don't take necessary risks. Don't ask.

OUTCOMES

Slow and painful idea/vision death.

That said, if not you, then who? If not now, then when? Do you think you'd be the first person to lose a donor or investor's money or "waste" their time? (I put waste in quotation marks because I don't believe in waste. If you learn, nothing is ever wasted.) Risk is an inherent part of ideas. The importance of failure is only whether it causes you to quit moving forward with your ideas or how you used it to learn and move forward.

The ultimate risk with this view is that you'll eventually abandon your idea because you don't have enough faith in yourself or your idea to move it forward.

The Two Simple Steps to Disempower Limiting Views

Once you know what your baggage is, what do you do with it?

- **No. 1.** Your first option is to consciously shift your view from a limiting one to a positive one, and drive your actions off of that view. For example, if my view is 'it's not okay to ask for money,' a possible alternate view would be that 'asking for money is a necessary part of the success of any idea.' Then, my actions would mirror that it's a necessary step, and I would make a plan to ask for money.

- **No. 2.** Your second option to shift a limiting view is to write a commitment that you'll stick to no matter how you feel or what the view tells you to do. For example, if my view is that 'it's not okay to fail,' I may write and follow a commitment that states that I will continue to work on my idea no matter how many times I fail.

 ## Steps to Success - Making your Big Idea Happen Right Now!

Are you starting to see a trend in your own views? Every one of them impacts your ability to succeed with your ideas. These self-defeating views are insidious, because they literally control every action, limiting what comes out of our mouths and driving astonishing self-fulfilling failures as our outcomes. When you hear the voice that says *don't ask* or *don't do* ringing inside your head, grab a pen and your notebook. Identify the view and try on a more supportive view, or make a commitment that will stand despite that view.

SUCCESS STORIES FROM IDEA LEADERS

Jamie Traeger-Muney, PhD, Founding Partner, Wealth Legacy Group LLC

Emily Bouchard, MSSW, Managing Partner, Wealth Legacy Group LLC

D r. Jamie Traeger-Muney is a psychologist who specializes in wealth psychology and Bowenian family systems. She was the first psychologist ever hired by a bank (Wells Fargo) to provide services to ultra-high net worth families. Emily Bouchard is the author of *Estate Planning for the Blended Family* and founder of Blended-Families LLC, specializing in the unique dynamics of blended families where there are children, step-children and step-parents, as well as a partner in the Wealth Legacy Group. Both Jamie and Emily are Certified Money Coaches and understand the money baggage we all carry.

Q: What sparked the idea that became the Wealth Legacy Group?

A: Dr. Traeger-Muney: I started the business right after I finished my PhD program in clinical psychology. I was very interested in conversations that weren't being had around money. I noticed people weren't talking about money except when they didn't have enough money. When there was sufficient money or plenty of money, that conversation was noticeably absent. That made me very curious. I have a philosophy that any conversation that isn't happening is somewhat like the stuff you leave in the back of the fridge and forget about. It can become moldy and disgusting. When we don't have conversation about an issue, we don't have the opportunity to freely express all different kinds of feelings around an issue, and it can get really gnarly.

Q: So you had an observation of discomfort around money. How did that turn into an entire business of helping families work through money issues?

A: Dr. Traeger-Muney: I felt like I wanted to be entrepreneurial, and when I finished my PhD I believed I had a lot of expertise. What I didn't have was a real business sense or knowledge of how to really launch a business. I took this great class that was called The Business of Psychology, and one of the first things they said was that psychologists tend to not be memorable, and that we all tend to specialize in general topics like anxiety or depression. They said the more you can find a specific niche, then the more you can focus your energy and become an expert in that niche, and the more you would get to be known. I started to think about some

> The more you can find a specific niche, then the more you can focus your energy and become an expert in that niche, and the more you would get to be known.

of the topics that interested me, and money was one of them. I felt like this was the most unique thing to pursue. I really wanted to be able to help people talk about the things that weren't being talked about.

Q: When you came up with this idea, what were all the little voices in your head that you had to deal with? What kind of stuff came up for you, and how did you move through it so you could move forward?

A: Dr. Traeger-Muney: I have a very supportive family, but both my parents had a strong reaction to what I wanted to do. When I first told my mother, who is also a psychologist that I was going to specialize in this area, her first reaction was, "Please don't tell my friends." My father, who is a business man, said 'what do you have to offer this clientele?' It really called upon me to stand in what I did have to bring and what I did have to offer and there was a lot of baggage in there that could have stopped me I think being in a structured class with mentors who were really helping me made a huge difference, as I know I am a person who works best in collaboration [with others]. So, I really went out and sought out partnerships to keep me from being stopped in my idea.

Q: When you come up with an idea, one of the biggest hurdles people encounter is being able to

communicate it in a way that people really get it. So how did both of you craft and hone a message so that people were engaged and wanting to work with you?

> We speak to who we serve and what we can do for them. This immediately brings people to a place where they go, "I need your services," or, "I know exactly who could use those services."

A: Ms. Bouchard: It's a very interesting field. One of the things we discovered is we're much more effective when we speak about the challenges of the people we work with, and what happens to them as a result. So instead of saying we're wealth psychologists and we work in the field of the emotional side of money, we would say well, if a couple is dealing with significant differences in terms of how much money or wealth they're bringing into the relationship, we can help them navigate their conversation so that it strengthens their marriage rather than cracks the foundation. We speak to who we serve and what we can do for them. This immediately brings people to a place where they go, "I need your services," or, "I know exactly who could use those services."

A: Dr. Traeger-Muney: There is this piece around being a champion. Early on in the practice I had this woman leave me a prank call. She was saying, "Therapy for wealthy people, really? That's what you do? Are you kidding me?" She saw my website and felt so strongly she felt she had to call and leave her name and number and it really made me think, why am I doing this?

I love having the ability to help others clear their money baggage, and then they can make huge changes. They can leverage their wealth and leverage their connections to make huge, positive changes in the world. That was something I got very excited about. Instead of something to be ashamed of or embarrassed about, this idea was something that I could be excited about that I could position myself and really leverage my own value, introducing lots of shifts and changes that were really important to my goals in making the world a better place.

Q: You did choose an area that carries a lot of baggage with it. You took something that people don't want to talk about. Why do people have that kind of baggage around money?

A: Ms. Bouchard: We could write a whole book on money, and many have written books on it. The short answer to that is, the one relationship we have in our lives that is the most misunderstood and the most universal, and that we have to deal with every single day, is our relationship with money. Despite that, we don't have any consistent competencies and role modeling around money that allow us to thrive.

So the people who have challenges have historical relationship patterns, what they have seen, what they have heard, what has been done in relationship to money that shaped who they are in their own relationship to money. We work with all types of patterns related to money in order to help people understand this so that they don't get caught up thinking it's personal. There are eight common money traits, and they have been extensively researched— and they're universal. I talk about them in my book, *Estate Planning for the Blended Family*. Helping people understand how universal money issues are is extraordinarily helpful, because it shows them that they can break free of that, and be happy with how they're moving with money. They have other options and choices they can draw on.

Q: You have had things go wrong with your teams and now you have things going right. What advice would you give to someone around building the right team to make an idea happen?

A: Dr. Traeger-Muney: When I look back on my first partnership, no one liked this person, and I have never had people in my life have such a strong reaction to one person in my life where I didn't listen. I think there were two things at play for me that made me not listen. I wanted a partner that was strong. I also think there was this piece, and like a marriage they say don't go into it thinking you're going to change that person.

> Looking at a business partnership is really looking at it like a marriage, and you don't want to rush into it; you really want to find out who that person is. You want to know where the challenges are, and if there is a sense that something isn't right then you have to listen to your gut.

I think there was a part of me that thought if I could help this person have a different and successful experience with partnership, that she was going to be different. That was really altruistic of me, but it didn't serve our partnership and what our partnership was about, and it didn't serve me or what I wanted to ultimately accomplish.

A: Ms. Bouchard: Looking at a business partnership is really looking at it like a marriage, and you don't want to rush into it; you really want to find out who that person is. You want to know where the challenges are, and if there is a sense that something isn't right then you have to listen to your gut. You need to be able to see that you can work through those things. Jamie and I worked together at another consultancy, and we really hit it off.

We had a great time working together. We got to know each other on a whole other level. As we grew in our relationship and we got to know each other, and as she started looking at making a major move to another country, we got into conversation and we used this energy leadership training program (www.energyforsuccess.org) to really empower us. I could be a managing partner in the US, and she could get her legs on the ground in Israel, and the company could continue to grow and thrive. It's really been an incredible journey.

Q: How long did it take before you had clients?

A: Dr. Traeger-Muney: The clients started coming fairly quickly, and that is one of the neat things about being in a niche profession—we get so many people who find us from the Internet. A) we're doing something unique and, B) even in that unique field we're covering from a unique perspective that particularly speaks to inheritors and women and couples and blended families, which are more specialty areas.

A: Ms. Bouchard: We were also given good advice from a mentor who has been in this field for a long time. I was feeling done with the other company I was working for, and Jamie and I were just getting started. He said, "No, don't quit your day job," and he was really clear about that. Make sure you have yourself covered as you're going forward, and do it incrementally. And as you see it building, then you can shift to working full-time on the idea. I think some people fail because they put everything into it and they overextend themselves, and then it takes longer than they anticipated.

Q: It sounds like it was a good five years to build the idea into a business. Would that be accurate?

A: Dr. Traeger-Muney: Yes, and I would also say there is a certain type of temperament to being in an entrepreneurial endeavor that not everybody has, and I think it's really important for people when they're thinking about an idea to really assess, "Am I the kind of person who likes the ups and downs, who can handle the uncertainty, or not?" Be honest with yourself, because the last thing you want to do is go into it and then look back and say, "What was I thinking? I never had the stomach for this."

A: Ms. Bouchard: If you have a great idea that's excellent, and you need to be aware that as you are just starting out, you need to have solid business understanding. The Small Business Administration is an incredible resource. They give amazing free consulting to really support you in your success. I think a lot of people have great ideas, and then they can get sucked in by a lot of entrepreneurial training that might be much more expensive than they need.

BUILD YOUR PLAN

"Planning is bringing the future into the present so that you can do something about it now."

- Alan Lakein

I am a planning addict. I schedule every hour of my life as far as I can figure it out, given the information I have and the goals I want to accomplish. I schedule everything on my computer calendar, including the time I will exercise, take vacations, eat my meals, do my meditation, and call my mom.

Planning my time and what I do with that time is why I believe I feel so fulfilled in my life. Contrary to what some people may perceive, planning gives you freedom, not constraint.

Contrary to what some people may perceive, planning gives you freedom, not constraint.

I plan my vacation. That way I get my down time. I schedule my focus time for work so that I don't let my day get taken away from me by e-mail, meetings, Facebook, or one of the thousand other electronic distractions life now brings us. I schedule marketing time so I keep a steady flow of work coming into my organization to ensure I don't go out of business.

You want to become a master at keeping your ideas alive and in business, too. Your idea will definitely require a plan. Most ideas can be managed by a simple plan. I manage almost all of my ideas via an electronic calendar function, a spreadsheet, and a giant wall calendar which visually shows all my big deliverables. Some of your ideas are complex and will have many parts; in that case, a more formal plan may be required.

The intent of this practice is not to write a long chapter on project planning. There are over a million resources on the internet on how to write a plan. The Plan It practice is instead about getting clear on how to take the idea to a commitment, how to take your commitment to goals, how to take action on your goals, and how to keep those actions happening in a specific time frame so you make progress.

The most important thing to remember about your plan is captured by one of my favorite quotes from the movie *Varsity Blues*, "Things change, Mox." In the movie, Jonathan Moxon is a back-up quarterback with a pretty fun and easy life. His best friend, who is the star quarterback, is injured in a football accident, and Mox has to step up. His life changes overnight. With big ideas, your life can change instantaneously.

Plans are great and will form a framework to keep you moving forward on your idea. But, the plan is not set in stone. In some of the stories shared by the Idea Leaders in this book, some of them didn't end up with the same plan they started with, or even the same idea they started with. So it's important to plan, but be flexible and adaptable at the same time.

The basics steps in creating a plan are:

1. **State The Big Idea and Commitment**. This should already be captured and easy to copy from your *Mission to Million$ Journal* we discussed in Practice 2.

2. **Set your Goals**. Another easy win as we had you develop goals using Practice 2.

3. **Determine Actions.** For each goal that you list, you need to determine what actions you can take to make progress reaching that goal. It's often helpful to figure out what actions to take by thinking in a time range.

I recommend deciding on actions you can take in the next 30 days, the next 90 days, the next 6 months, and the next year initially and review quarterly thereafter.

4. **Identify Resources.** Ideas can rarely be accomplished by you alone. Look at what resources you'll need to get this done, thinking about time, supplies, real estate, insurance, consulting support, etc.

5. **Schedule Meetings.** If applicable to your idea, you may need to hold regular meetings to ensure the idea is moving forward.

6. **Select Your Team**. Who do you need to support you to get your idea done? What expertise do you need that you don't have now?

7. **Define Budget**. Most ideas cost money. How much do you need, and when do you need it by? If your idea requires fundraising, be sure you have captured that as a goal and created actions to support that goal.

8. **Create a Schedule**. Do you have a definite time you want to get your idea going and completed by? If you don't know, get started right now and set a deadline that is a stretch and makes you uncomfortable, and try it on. You will be surprised how much just setting a deadline will push you forward faster.

9. **Identify Metrics**. It's important to be able to show progress towards the realization of your Big Idea. How will you measure your progress? How will you know if each goal has been achieved? Thankfully, most metrics are very straightforward; but if yours are not, you may have to hire an expert to help you figure it out.

For most ideas, a simple planning template can be used. For Big Ideas happening in a larger context and setting, or those with more complexity, you may need to create detailed plans, as well as sub-plans, on such topics as risk control and communication. It can also help to use a project management tool such as Microsoft Project, Podio, or Basecamp.

Remember, the purpose of a plan is to hold yourself accountable, successfully execute your idea, and provide a clear framework that you and your team can follow. Secondarily, in some cases, your plan may be used as a funding tool (e.g., a business plan).

 ## Steps to Success - Making your Big Idea Happen Right Now!

Plans can sometimes feel onerous, so don't get overwhelmed too quickly. Pick one idea, and using the work you already completed in Practice 2 and the template provided, create a short plan to get it done. Set aside time each day to tackle an action on the plan. Even five minutes of action can keep an idea moving forward.

SAMPLE SIMPLE IDEA PLAN

Commitment Statement Written Across Top

Background:	Any key information you need to capture or others need to know
Goals:	1. Write your goals in this section
	2. Goal No. 2
	3. Goal No. 3
	4. Goal No. 4
Meetings:	What meetings do you ned to have to make the idea happen
Resources:	What resource do you need to make the idea happen (resources can be people, places, or things)
Budget:	What money to you need?
Project Start Date:	When will you start
Project End Date:	When will you be done
Project Team Lead:	Who will lead the team
Team Member:	Add members
Team Member:	Add members
Team Member:	Add members
Team Member:	Add members

Actions & Milestones:	GOAL NUMBER 1: xyz pdq	Metric(s)
Date 1	Action 1	
Date 2	Action 2	
Date 3	Action 3	
Date 4	Action 4	
Milestones:	GOAL NUMBER 2: xyz pdq	Metric(s)
Date 1	Action 1	
Date 2	Action 2	
Date 3	Action 3	

SUCCESS STORIES FROM IDEA LEADERS

Sylvia Heisey, Owner, Beets Cafe and Sylvia's Kitchen and Desserts

Sylvia Heisey took a personal interest in healthy food and created an entirely new career from it, completely unrelated to her original degree and career. She founded Beets Café out of a passion about healthful living and sharing it with the world. Including raw, living foods in her diet dramatically improved Sylvia's health and outlook on life. She opened a now nationally renowned raw food restaurant, and has since evolved that into a new business venture called Sylvia's Kitchen and Desserts.

Q: When you thought about opening Beets, what was the original idea that came into your head?

A: I was a consultant for sixteen years, and I traveled extensively. I had traveled to different countries and all around the US. I was exhausted, and tired of the travel. I was struggling with trying to justify my own health, my own well-being, and I wanted to help others be healthy and help them with their well-being. As part of my own recovery, I decided to change my diet and increase my exercise. During that process a couple of people mentioned raw food, so I decided to start doing some raw food.

> **You don't need to know, you just need to figure it out. You start your path and you start gathering the data. Just because you don't have experience and just because you haven't done it before, that doesn't mean you can't do something.**

As I was eating raw food, I was totally transformed. My body transformed, my disposition, and my clarity. Aches and pains that I had were gone. I started associating that with clean food. All of a sudden, I thought of all those people habitually taking medications to mask the issues of health. If they only knew about healthy living and about healthy, clean eating, that could change everything.

That is what sparked it. It was my own personal discovery about clean food and what it did for my body that helped me decide I needed to provide that to the community.

Q: So this was a total career shift for you. What were the first thoughts that came into your head?

A: One was, I have never done anything like this before. How am I going to do this? Do I have the energy for it, the physical energy for it? I knew it was going to be a lot of work, but I knew if I maintained the lifestyle of clean eating, then of course I would have the energy, because my energy shot through the roof! As far as not knowing what to do, that was also a path. I remember in a lecture I attended, my instructor mentioned that you don't need to know, you just need to figure it out. You start your path and you start gathering the data. Just because you don't have experience and just because you haven't done it before, that doesn't mean you can't do something.

You start to educate yourself, and you start figuring out what you need to do to make that dream a reality. So, I started gathering information about what it was going to take. Then, I decided I needed to go get certified as a raw food chef so I would have credibility and know what I was talking about. I was able to learn about the differences in nutrition, and learned how to develop different recipes and all the different aspects of creating this type of food.

Q: What was the first reaction you got from people when you shared your idea and what you were going to do? Was it positive, negative, a little of both?

A: It was a little bit of both. Some people said, "Wow, great idea! Austin [Texas] really needs something like this." Others said, "Oh, the restaurant business is so hard." I had both reactions.

Q: When you get these reactions, there is always your own baggage that you have to move out of the way in order to get moving forward. What do you feel your baggage was that you had to deal with?

A: I thought, how could I think that I could do this? What has me believe that I could actually get this thing going? Who am I to believe that I have what it takes? I had all of that.

Q: How did you build your team of support around your idea?

A: It was a lot of word of mouth. I did a lot of sharing about the idea, and it's interesting because it seemed to just happen in synchronicity. I met a woman at a festival in Sedona sharing about my idea. She called me and said, "I'm moving to Austin, and I'm a raw food chef who has taught at Culinary Arts for Raw Food. Do you need help?" I knew another young woman who was a hot shot administrative person who could start and set up anything if you just gave her the task. Luckily for me her job was ending, and I took her on.

Between the three of us developing recipes, and setting up policies and procedures, that was the beginning. The rest of it was an energy process. I started meeting other people through networks in similar circles around food, like a community farm event where I met local vendors. It was again that synchronistic energy that attracted the people whom I needed to know.

The other thing I was doing as a part of a kind of networking was that I was teaching classes way before the cafe opened around the development time. My whole idea was to teach and invite people who had large communities personally, so when I was ready to open, I was gathering people who were already in big communities so that the word could get out even more quickly.

Q: How long did it take from deciding to have a raw food restaurant to opening the doors of Beets?

A: Eight or nine months. I remember I was fooling around with this idea about doing this, and I would travel around and I would seek out raw food restaurants. I would observe, and I would ask to speak to the owners or managers. Sometimes they would invite me into the kitchen so I could take a look. There were different things like that, so I could gather data for myself.

Q: How long did you stay in that observation state versus taking action toward your plan?

My whole idea was to teach and invite people who had large communities personally, so when I was ready to open, I was gathering people who were already in big communities so that the word could get out even more quickly.

A: About six months. As I was thinking about whether or not I was going to do this, it came to me—somebody had to figure it out to begin with. Who started the first restaurant? They had to figure it out, and I can figure it out too, and make a plan.

Q: What kind of resistance and challenges came up along the way?

A: It was around the build-out of the location. Contractors, delays with permits, dealing with vendors, and in hindsight, I think I was a little too trusting. I should have been more rigorous in getting referrals, and getting a background on some people before I took them on.

Q: You have your first idea and then it changes, and you have to adapt it. Spend a couple of minutes talking about that as this idea has changed from its original form. How are you keeping your idea alive long term?

A: It's so important to write out a plan about the idea. Put your vision on paper, because there are so many possibilities that it's difficult to focus on what you originally thought you were going to do. I did that, so my own plan didn't change so much through the process. I knew I wanted to serve food, and I wanted to teach.

I think the biggest thing is when an idea comes up, write it down, get clear on what it is. Watch yourself, and don't move from that. The idea could go in many directions, and then there's not one thing that is focused, which can lead you off path. With a solid plan, you have to put your intention on one thing at a time, and then expand to some of the other ideas.

Q: If one of my readers had a Big Idea like yours and you could give one piece of advice, what do you think that would be?

A: Get clear about what it is you want to do. Be specific. What is the intent? What is the purpose? Make sure your business plan is consistent with that purpose.

BUILD YOUR TEAM

"Teamwork makes the dream work, but a vision becomes a nightmare when the leader has a big dream and a bad team."

- John C. Maxwell

I am a self-professed independent maverick. I love to work on my own. I can go days without talking to anyone when I'm in the thick of a good run on a project, idea, or book. But, I learned the hard way that you can't complete a project and not interact with a team, and you can't change the world with a great idea if you don't interact with the human race. And, the best ideas for making your idea happen probably won't come out of your own head. Thus the importance of surrounding yourself with a supportive team.

> **The best ideas for making your idea happen probably won't come out of your own head.**

In an ideal world, your team is a group of your #1 fans and relationship builders that bring specific skills to the table. Their skills complement yours, and they're willing to shamelessly promote and support your idea because they get it. They get at least ten times more out of their service than they put into it, whether that's money, energy, relationships, or learning. When teams work, they can become your 'mastermind' group, pushing your idea forward and constantly energizing and driving you to accomplish your mission.

In reality, many teams are made up of well-meaning people who have an unclear idea about what they should be doing and what their collective role really is. They aren't effective at staying strategically focused on the end-game (idea). So instead of being useful, they can become a drag on your idea. They can stifle vision and innovation, and focus on self-preservation and survival.

How do you get the former outcome to help you move your idea forward versus the latter outcome? Start looking at your team like a mentoring group. Being on a team is an opportunity to interact with a group of peers, who each bring their expertise to deliver on an idea, and who should be helpful in building relationships that ensure delivery of the idea.

At the end of the day, in order to bring an idea into reality, it's essential to have a team of people who are supportive, accountable and committed. Whether you're launching a new company, revitalizing an existing one, building a Non-Profit Organization (NPO), or just getting a Big Idea to launch across a large company or community, your team is an essential tool.

Choosing team members wisely makes good business sense, as it will impact your ability to raise funds, make connections, build relationships and obtain funding quickly. So, who do you want on your team?

Choose people with integrity who are:

- Not intimidated by straight talk and who communicate directly

- Focused on outcomes

- Highly competent in their areas of expertise

- Ready to tackle complex problems, sort through them, and enjoy doing it

- Optimists and realists who have the temperament to overcome obstacles, not quit or become the naysayer

- Enthusiastic and have a great sense of humor (believe

me, keeping the fun while getting to your vision comes in handy)

- Open-minded and don't rapidly jump to conclusions

In addition to the personality traits listed above, you're also looking to bring people to your team who bring new areas of expertise to your idea—areas that you may be lacking yourself.

8 Steps to Identify the Right Team

Step 1: Decide What you Need

This should include an honest evaluation of the skills you have to personally deliver on your idea. Then list any additional skills that you'll need to complete the competencies you require.

Step 2: Make a List of Your Dream Team

Compare them against your skills from Step 1 and the personality traits you want. Don't just ask people you like. Ask people you respect.

Step 3: Work Your Network

Think wide and broad on who you know. You'll be looking at your co-workers, friends, schoolmates, clients, customers, vendors, and social acquaintances. You'll be surprised at how many great team members reside in your LinkedIn, Facebook, Twitter, and other social media networks.

> **You'll be surprised at how many great team members reside in your LinkedIn, Facebook, Twitter, and other social media networks.**

Step 4: Remember that Bigger is Not Necessarily Better

Keep your team size manageable. The smaller your team, the more efficiently it will operate. When teams grow larger than 6-8 people, they become significantly harder to manage.

Step 5: Be Honest. Money Does Matter

In your skills list, it's important to have someone who's skilled at fundraising. You need at least one person who knows how to raise capital, whether money, resources, or people, depending on what your idea requires. Even if you feel like you may not need capital right away, you will.

Step 6: Don't Forget Legalities, Politics and Other Sundry Items

Depending on what type of team you're assembling, there are ethical and legal issues. I knew a doctor who had changed

> **You should spend as much time selecting your team as you would hiring an employee or contractor. They can be the catalyst that pushes your idea faster and further than you ever could yourself, or they can be the anchor that holds you back.**

careers, but kept his medical license. He got in trouble with the American Medical Association for endorsing a product, which, in this case, was not legal for him to do as a doctor. So, fully understanding any legal implications of your idea is an area in which you need to be educated. Many times you have to pay for legal advice, but first check with your local Small Business Administration, which may be able to provide you with legal advice or resources for free.

Step 7: Take Your Time

You should spend as much time selecting your team as you would hiring an employee or contractor. They can be the catalyst that pushes your idea faster and further than you ever could yourself, or they can be the anchor that holds you back.

Step 8: Enroll Them in Your Possibility

Individuals capable of providing strong mentorship and leadership are typically busy people who participate in a lot of things. You'll need to recruit them to want to be a part of your idea! So go back to Practice 3 and make sure you have your one-minute mission message (OM³) ready to engage and enroll your team members.

At the end of the day, follow these steps as a guide to picking your team, but also follow your intuition. Many of my clients reported to me after the fact that they knew they shouldn't choose a particular person, but they ignored their intuition and did it anyway.

Steps to Success - Making your Big Idea Happen Right Now!

Take a close, hard look at your idea. Make a list of the skills needed—in addition to your own—to build a great team to support this idea. Then, scroll through all your networks: social, family, work, community, church, and virtual, to see who might have the skills you identified. Set a schedule of when you'll invite each person to help you make your idea happen, and set a date by when you'll have your entire team convened. This will hold you accountable to making it happen. Last, but not least, be clear on what you require from them as a team member. Clear expectations and communication make productive team members.

SUCCESS STORIES FROM IDEA LEADERS

Rachel Gutter, Director, Center for Green Schools

The Center for Green Schools at the U.S. Green Building Council (USGBC) was established in 2010 to serve as the driver for green schools dialogue, policy development and innovation. With its start, the USGBC appointed Rachel Gutter to lead the center and make its Big Idea happen. Rachel came to the USGBC in 2007 to oversee the launch of LEED for Schools, a version of USGBC's popular green building certification program that facilitates the design, construction and operations of high-performance, green schools.

Today, Ms. Gutter is widely regarded as one of the nation's foremost experts on the topic of green schools. More than 100 major media outlets have sought Rachel's perspective, including the *Washington Post*, the *New York Times*, *USA Today* and CNN. In 2011, she was honored as an eco-heroine in Martha Stewart's *Whole Living* magazine.

Q: What was the initial idea about starting a green schools movement?

A: I came to the USGBC in 2007, and my principal responsibility was to help to launch the LEED for Schools rating system, which was a green building rating system that was tailored specifically to meet the needs of K–12 school environments. We started to understand that healthy children who are prepared for a bright future is a universal value that everyone shares. We realized using schools as an entry point for a larger conversation about green building was an amazing way to get people who would otherwise be resistant to conversations about green, about sustainability, about LEED certification, to really pay attention. By 2010, we had a dozen different programs or initiatives we were working on inside USGBC related to green schools.

Q: What happened next?

A: Creating the school was the idea of Roger Platt, who is our Senior Vice President of Global Policy and Law. He wandered into my CEO Rick Fedrizzi's office one day and he said, "What if we took all the work we're doing on green schools and established a Center for Green Schools to really solidify USGBC's leadership around the topic? The center could create a much more powerful platform for all of our communities, and send a message to the world that where our children learn matters." Rick called me into his office that day and said, "You have the weekend to put a business plan together for this thing we are going to call the Center for Green Schools, and then we're going to go out and raise several million dollars for it." In six months, that is exactly what we did.

Q: How did you make that idea happen that fast?

A: We did a couple of really critical things, that looking back, I'm not sure how intentional or how insistent I would have been on them happening, but thank God that we made those choices when we did.

The first thing that happened was we made a decision to change the mission statement we first started with, which was "Green Schools within a generation" to "Green schools within *this* generation." So, in 2010 we started the countdown. We said that when the kindergartners of today have kindergartners of their own, that's the deadline we're going to meet to ensure that every child attends a school that is healthy, safe, and efficient.

The second thing we did was to go through a massive stakeholder alignment and engagement process in standing up the Center for Green Schools. It was probably the most comprehensive strategic planning process that USGBC had undertaken in recent years. We did

We did dozens upon dozens of stakeholder interviews and visioning sessions. By the time we were ready to launch the Center for Green Schools, we had a tremendous amount of buy-in and support.

dozens upon dozens of stakeholder interviews and visioning sessions. By the time we were ready to launch the Center for Green Schools, we had a tremendous amount of buy-in and support, as well as a lot of people who felt like they have been there with us from the beginning.

Q: How did you attract so much funding and so many great partners?

A: I was very insistent that our relationships with our sponsors and funders would be somewhat non-traditional; I wanted to work with our funders and sponsors as strategic partners. When a Fortune 50 company agrees to provide the seed money you need to get an initiative off the ground then guess what—fifteen minutes of strategizing with the Chief Sustainability Officer of a Fortune 50 company is as valuable as the donation of money.

We worked very hard to create a strategic partnership with United Technologies and, since then, with all of our other strategic partners and funders. This means it cuts both ways. We just worked with one of our other partners, Interface Flooring, who are well known for their immense achievements around sustainability and green manufacturing. We helped them redesign their sales strategy for the K–12 market. It's a symbiotic relationship.

Q: Can you talk about some of the things, or voices in your head that could have taken you down or slowed you down, and how you quieted those voices?

A: First of all, I think I had inexperience on my side. I didn't know enough to be afraid. Amongst our partners and peers, the Center for Green Schools is known for being fearless. We just jumped in and we were not afraid of the enormity of the task. We estimated that just to bring K–12 US public schools to a place where they meet today's education, health, and safety standards, it would take a minimum of $542 billion dollars of investment. That is enough to stop anyone in their tracks. But, we just jumped in head first, and we did not allow ourselves to be afraid.

Our goal is to fund ourselves through channels that are distinct from our peer organizations. We believe that it is really hard to be a great partner to someone if you are vying for the same pot of money and being a great partner is our highest priority.

Q: When you first shared this idea, what was the reaction?

A: One of the biggest issues in the nonprofit universe, particularly in the environmental arena, is that there are so few funding resources and so many entities competing for that funding. Oftentimes, even though we know that in order to tackle the challenges that we are attempting to solve that we need more people and more organizations to engage, we nonetheless feel threatened by new personalities and players. We push them out of the equation, we don't invite them to have a seat at the table, because we think they are going to come in and take our money and our resources and our visibility.

We definitely experienced some of this resistance in the beginning and that significantly influenced our fund development strategy. Our goal is to fund ourselves through channels that are distinct from our peer organizations. We believe that it is really hard to be a great partner to someone if you are vying for the same pot of money and being a great partner is our highest priority.

Q: One of the things you did really well was that you crafted a very clear message and verbalized what you were doing. What did it take to create that?

A: I think it took us a long time to hit it on the head. I remember just being so frustrated with myself for not being able to get out of building, architecture, engineer 'nerd speak.' My commitment to being accurate was overriding my desire to be able to communicate with a broader audience than just green building practitioners. The most helpful exercise we ever went through was when we were preparing to launch our Green Apple Day of Service – a day when everyone, parents, community members, students, teachers, can get involved in the good work of transforming their schools.

In preparation to launch the Green Apple brand, we conducted a number of consumer focus groups. Of course, focus groups are business as usual for for-profit companies that market directly to consumers, but it is not something I had ever heard of another nonprofit doing to tailor its messaging around a new initiative. It was so helpful, every single message that we tested that I predicted would be a lead contender, failed miserably. For instance, we found out that parents don't like to be hit with any messaging that implies that they have yet another problem to worry about when it comes to raising healthy, successful kids. The messaging we found that was most effective for reaching moms and dads had everything to do with tapping into their desire to give their children that one extra opportunity to succeed. What parent won't go to great lengths to do that?

We nonprofits can really take an important cue from for-profits, particularly from those that are marketing to consumers, and what they do with focus groups to be sure their messaging resonates with their target audience.

Q: What would your advice be to others who are looking to turn their Big Idea into reality?

A: Be fearless. Whether you may fail or not, doesn't really matter, it's the attitude with which you approach a new opportunity that matters. We tried a lot of things that didn't work at the center, but nobody looks back and says, "Boy, that Center for Green Schools was a big failure".

It's also important to empower your people and your partners. I am adamant that every member of the Center team has ownership within their own universe. We empower our volunteers in the same way. I think that so often in our attempt to start something new, we try to tightly contain it, and I'm not sure that's the way you birth a new idea. And I'm sure that's not the way you birth a new movement.

Lastly, it's extremely important to define the metrics and milestones for your success, track your progress toward those goals and revisit them frequently. We had to get comfortable holding our feet to the fire in reaching some very aggressive and ambitious aspirations and be brave enough to be transparent about where we are in reaching those goals. I encourage people to think about how they can make visible their progress and do that in a way that resonates authentically with their mission, with their culture and with their stakeholders.

BUILD YOUR CASE

"When it is obvious that the goals cannot be reached, don't adjust the goals, adjust the action steps."

- Confucius

In this chapter, we will talk about taking your idea and selling it in a more formal fashion, in what is called a case for action. In the simplest terms, a case for action is a document in which the end result inspires the reviewer or reader to take a specific action related to your idea. There is a clear request made by you and clear action provided to the receiver of the document so the person is clear on how they can successfully support you and your idea.

> **In the simplest terms, a case for action is a document in which the end result inspires the reviewer or reader to take a specific action related to your idea.**

I recommend you create a case for action, because it forces you to get disciplined and focused about your message beyond your 60-second OM³ messages you created to share your idea in Practice 3: Communicate. In the formal business sense, a case for action is sometimes referred to as 'case statements' (common in the NPO world) or 'business proposals' (more common in the for-profit world). But, more simply, a case can be the flyer you hand out at a community gathering, or an e-mail to a specific target group. The only difference is usually the length and level of detail provided.

Your case for action (i.e., that which gets people to take an action around your idea) should be inherent in all of your written communications, such as:

- E-mails

- Blogs

- Elevator Speeches (Your 60-second idea share)

- Proposals

- Presentations

- Status and Annual Reports

- Social Media (Twitter, LinkedIn, Facebook, Google+, Pinterest and so on)

- QR Codes

- iPhone and Smartphone Apps

- Websites

In my experience, most business proposals and case statements fail for three key reasons. Most commonly, the request or action you want the reader to take is absent, or buried in a bunch of adjectives and adverbs.

The second most common reason the case fails is because the action requested is made too difficult to fulfill, or the steps are so unclear that people reading (or listening) can't even pay attention to what they're reading or seeing.

The third reason a case will fail is it's a bunch of 'blah blah blah' and not much else. Studies have shown that technology is changing our brains, specifically in the areas of how we perceive and read and remember things. In the article "The Internet has become the External Hard Drive for our Memories", Daniel M. Wegner and Adrian F. Ward explored the phenomenon of how th einternet is affecting our ability to recall and retain information.[5] Any non-memorable 'blah blah blah' is a death knell on a case for action, as we're all becoming people who read for sound-bites and have shorter attention spans. Here are two concepts to keep in mind as general guidelines to follow overall.

Talk about the people you're serving and the value you're creating. Your job is to connect your idea to what people need

---

5- Wegner, Daniel M. & Ward, Adrian F. (2013) "The Internet Has Become the External Hard Drive for Our Memories", Scientific American. 19 Nov 2013.

and value. You have to find where your idea impacts people and talk from that point of view.

Passion matters. Facts are overrated: People spend their money emotionally, not cerebrally. As an engineer who really believed I made all my decisions based on fact, and controlled my emotions like Spock on *Star Trek*, this was a difficult concept for me to believe. The most fascinating study I found showed that brain injury patients who'd had the emotion part of their brain taken out in an accident couldn't make any decisions, no matter how many facts they were given.[6-7]

> There are many visionaries who don't have their facts and business plan neatly lined up, but they still make huge social changes and launch amazingly successful businesses, because they're a charismatic leader and have a compelling story in their case for action.

Facts do have their place, but they're not the main reason people will follow your idea; they just reinforce a decision already made. I remember meeting with a large group of venture capitalists and interviewing them to understand why

6 - Camp, Jim, (2012) "Decisions Are Emotional, not Logical: The Neuroscience behind Decision Making.", 11 June 2012.

7 - Damasio, Antonio (1994). "Descartes' Error - Emotion, Reason, and the Human Brain".

they decided to fund an idea. The group's CEO told me that they first looked for a charismatic leader, then a compelling story, *then* they checked out the facts. Without the first two, the facts alone were never enough for them to invest in a big idea. There are many visionaries who don't have their facts and business plan neatly lined up, but they still make huge social changes and launch amazingly successful businesses, because they're a charismatic leader and have a compelling story in their case for action. A case for action can be completed in eight simple steps.

Designing a Case for Action (CFA)

Step 1: Begin with the end in mind

Similar to the OM^3 conversation you crafted in Practice 3, write the case for action with the outcome in mind. Possible uses for a case for action could be to:

- *Get a Commitment:* Getting someone to make a commitment to do something

- *Influence a View or Trigger an Action:* Direct them toward a certain action or viewpoint

- *Educate:* Communicate your programs and goals and gain their understanding and participation in what you're doing.

- ***Get Their Endorsement***: Have them sign on and say they're behind you. Gives you credibility.

- ***Recruit Them***: Get them to be part of what you're doing as an investor, donor, volunteer, board member, or team member.

- ***Prospect:*** Reach out to people and get their expert opinions on what you're doing, even before it is formally out in the community or marketplace. People love to give their opinions and expertise.

- ***Create a Foundation:*** This document lays the foundation for all the other things you have to send out. It forms the framework so you have consistent messaging across all of your communication and marketing channels.

Step 2: Grab them at hello

Titles matter. If you learn anything in marketing, learn what types of statements and wording get people's attention from the beginning. The title will keep them reading. Which statement below are you more likely to read?

"Amazing weight loss plan" or "Lose 20 pounds in 20 days"

"Building green communities through generations" or "Your house is making you sick"

Be fearless about having people give input on your titles. There are lots of customer relationship management software tools now you can use which allow you to try different titles on the same case for action to see which email gets opened more (this is called a 'split test').

Step 3: Keep them reading

Tell a story. Use an attention-grabbing statistic. Ask a question. The best copywriters say that you spend 80 percent of your time writing the first few sentences or paragraphs of a document and 20 percent on the rest. I personally can attest to that, as my goal is to keep the person you want to take action reading past the first few sentences. One way to keep people reading is to ask a question. Who LOVES to get answers to a question? You do!

Step 4: Make your case

I have seen this done through both hard facts and engaging stories. Either can work, but make sure you test it on the desired audience before you plan an entire marketing campaign!

Case for Action: Fact-based approach

On the example here using a fact-based approach, the goal was to make companies aware that their buildings were having a very negative impact on the health of their occupants. So in this case for action, the organization chose a fact-based approach:

Example: Construction Company

Did you know that one in five people is subjected to Sick Building Syndrome (SBS)? Attributed to poor ventilation, poor building design, and high levels of pollution and humidity, it results in a 14% decrease in productivity and millions of hours of lost sick time at work and school.

Did you know that buildings produce 65% of all waste in the US every year? That's 143 MM tons of waste annually—enough to cover the entire state of Texas!

Did you know that asthma is the most common chronic disease in children, and is the third-ranking cause of hospitalization in children ages 15 and younger?

Did you know that your home, office, or school could be making you sick?

Case for Action: Story-based approach

In the following example, the goal was to inspire the funder to stop viewing this non-profit organization as a think tank and instead view it as an organization that builds leaders who change the world, so they chose a story-based approach.

Example: Non-profit Leadership Academy

In 2001, Joe attended an Emerging Professionals chapter meeting. He confesses that he lurked in the back of the meetings, not knowing where he fit. Fast forward to 2011. Through participation in our leadership development academy, he has evolved into one of our most influential leaders. Joe founded his chapter's Emerging Professionals group, and rallied the area's young adults to participate in community building projects. Having had no advocacy experience, Joe learned from our program how to drive green legislation, convince an influential developer to design a large, publically funded project, and John helped draft the city's healthy building tax statement, which grants tax exemptions for any certified property valued at $500,000 or less. He has built coalitions between unions, NPOs, politicians, and businesses.

Not only did the Emerging Professional's leadership development program pull Joe from lurking in the back, but it kept his talents and passion in his home town, Cincinnati, instead of moving to 'greener environmental pastures' in Seattle. Joe says, "If everyone who thought and believed like me moved away to other greener cities, who would be left to help change the rest of the country? Moving away now seems like retreating from the challenge. Seattle is doing just fine without me."

Step 5: Why you? Share your uniqueness, your history, your mission and your idea

If you did your job in Steps 1–4, now people want to know about you and your organization, your history, how you came to be, your mission and your Big Idea. They now want to connect with the people (remember, it's about the people) who have created this amazing idea. It's fine to talk about the organization in the "Why you" conversation, but remember that an organization is made up of people. Talking about "Why you" should emphasize your value and uniqueness so they're confident your idea for a product, service, or big, world-changing mission will be here to stay. As Jim Collins, one of my favorite authors wrote an entire book about, you get to show that you're *Built to Last*.

Step 6: Create urgency - Why them? Why now?

We all want to be appreciated and recognized for what we bring to the table. Yet many cases for action have such broad appeal that we don't see how we fit into and align with what you're proposing. This is where you make it 100% clear why them and why now. Capture the urgency and possibility of what could happen, and that it needs to happen now.

Step 7: How will it be done?

This is where the business, budget, cost and other facts show you're not providing just a bunch of pretty language and a good marketing pitch. People want to know that you have a plan to get there. This section can be as short as one paragraph for a simple case for action, and pages long for a business plan proposal or a big funding request. Above all, this section should show that you have an outcome you want to produce, and a way you think it can be produced.

WARNING: It's normal to get really hung up and insecure at this part of a call for action. You may have thoughts running in your head like, "I have no clue how this will happen," or, "I'm really not sure how to do this," or, "What if what I put in here ends up being a complete load of bull?"

Here is the reality: You'll lean on your team and thought leaders for this part. As I mentioned before, the best ideas and plans to get your idea to happen may not come from you. Do your research. Talk to people with experience around your idea. Find people who have implemented similar ideas and see what worked for them.

A second reality check is that plans change all the time. Some ideas are so big you can only figure out the first few steps. It's okay to not have 100 percent of the answers. Lay out what you think, and then stay in communication as things change.

Step 8: Clear request and call to action

Step 8 is where the rubber meets the road. It's where you should have a clear action that you want your target audience to take as a result, and lay it out so it's easy to say yes. Wherever possible, provide an incentive to encourage them to say yes. If it's a simple request, then it could be a sentence with a hyperlink to a website, or phone number, or form to fill out. But, it must be a specific and clear action. Seth Godin talks about when your customer (or gorilla) is ready, the first thing they're going to say is "Where's the banana?" In a case for action, when the target audience says, "Great, let's go, where is the action?", it has better be there. Keep it clean and simple. If it has to be a complex request, it should be laid out in clear steps and simple terms. There should be no confusion about what you want them to do.

Is the Case for Action good, and is it done? The Litmus Test

That's it—you're almost done. Now comes test time. How do you test your case for action? Here are a few things you can do to see if you've got it.

- **Keep it short and simple and ban jargon**. Jerold Panas, who is a well-known fundraiser in the non-profit world, tells a great story about a mentor making him cross out all the adjectives and adverbs in his Case for Action, and then see if the content still stands. This is an awesome practice, and it works. We tend to use adjectives and adverbs to gloss over the fact we're missing critical content. Don't fall into that trap.

- **Make it clear**. Use anyone who is willing to read it as an editor. If they don't understand what you've said, other people probably won't either.

- **If it's boring to you, it's boring to them, too**. Leave out the parts the reader will skip! I can easily tell which parts my readers will skip because when I review them, I don't want to read them either. Leave them out. If you read it and don't want to finish reading, they won't either. We often write too much. Shorten it up and get a fresh set of eyes on it.

- **Is the outcome clear?** Remember, Step 1 in crafting the case for action was to start with the end in mind. Be sure that the document should start by talking about the endpoint and the 'why', not the 'how' and means to get there. We don't need to know all the steps it took to get there, just the outcome and the value of that outcome.

- **Is the call to action simple?** The simplest, most focused requests produce the best results. Succinctly tell your reader what you want them to do in clear direct action.

- **Are you a Negative Nelly?** Attitude is contagious. A negative call to action could result in a negative reaction. Ensure that you convey a positive message that leaves the reader empowered and wanting to take action, not stuck in resignation and inaction.

 ## Steps to Success - Making your Big Idea Happen Right Now!

Look back at your OM^3 you created in Practice 3. Carefully consider your target audience(s). Focus on putting one good case for action together for your No. 1 target audience. Then adapt your case for action you develop as needed for the rest of your potential audiences.

SUCCESS STORIES FROM IDEA LEADERS

Microsoft Project Spark Team

Henry Sterchi, Creative Director, Team Dakota (Project Spark) Microsoft Studios

Every video gamer anxiously awaits the release dates when Microsoft announces a new game platform. How do they keep creating amazing ideas that engage and inspire over and over again? I interviewed Henry Sterchi with Microsoft's Team Dakota, the idea makers behind Project Spark, and they peeled back the veil to give us a look at how they took a brand new concept for gaming, different from their core products, and made it happen in a high-pressure and highly competitive marketplace.

Q: What did the idea of Project Spark look like when it was originally conceived—was it even called Project Spark?

A: We worked with a variety of possible names. Ultimately, we wanted something that could capture the limitless imagination and the collaboration of the always evolving nature of our game, so we landed with Project Spark.

For your readers who are not familiar with the Project Spark, it includes a simple to learn, but robust visual programming language that is derived from a Microsoft Research (MSR) Project called Kodu. The core concept focused on providing a way for the masses to make their own games. We combined a 2.0 version of Kodu that was upgraded and highly customized to support specific game functions with a powerful voxel-based rendering engine that focused on a variety of "magical" sculpting, painting, and world-building tools to allow anyone to quickly make their own worlds, and then program anything in it.

The original prototype contained the ability to sculpt and paint the world, or to procedurally generate a world. Players could run around their world with a character, and enter the new version of Kodu to program things. We also included a "Biome," which combined creating the world and placing objects in one. The "hook and proof of concept" we used was that in 7 steps or less you could make a playable game.

Q: What made you take the next steps from idea to communicating it and moving it forward to a project?

A: We formed a very small team, which stayed heads down and focused on a very rapid prototype. The prototype was tested with the team and other various players, and ended up being successful in allowing a wide variety of players to make a game.

> **We did wonder how people would react to something that wasn't a game per se, and a concept that seemed like an impossible task in which we would "make a game that makes games".**

We would instantly see smiles and often hear gasps of "wow" from

> **We knew the first playable prototype had to absolutely nail it.**

players within even the first interaction. We saw a lot of these magic moments, from sculpting a little bit and then hitting test and seeing their world as they played in it, to the first time they programmed something and made it move or come to life. These moments really made us feel like we were onto something special.

Q: Once you knew you had an idea that you wanted to make happen at Microsoft, what were some of the little voices that came into your head about it?

A: There were several things that came to mind. The first notions were what technologies and platforms were Microsoft Studios developing that would allow us to execute best on our vision. We quickly realized that if we wanted everyone to make games, being both on personal computer (PC) and Console would be very important. We were also very excited about using Kinect, Mouse and Keyboard, Touch, and Controllers for input and output.

We did wonder how people would react to something that wasn't a game per se, and a concept that seemed like an impossible task in which we would "make a game that makes games."

We knew the first playable prototype had to absolutely nail it.

Q: What was the first reaction of people when you shared it initially with the folks that you needed to have support it?

A: There were a lot of smiles and a lot of disbelief. One of the keys of Project Spark is that you can basically do anything you can imagine. So we'd spend the beginning of the demo showing the capabilities and letting people try it. It would quickly turn into a series of can it do this or that. We would then show them that you could, which would lead them to challenge us further. It would almost turn into a game of stump Project Spark, and we would often find ourselves in 2- and 3-hour demos instead of the planned 30 minutes to an hour!

Q: What baggage or resistance did you have to get a handle on as a team that had to be moved out of the way to move Project Spark forward?

A: Most of the early hurdles on the prototype were technical, and involved some great coordination with various groups around Microsoft to align and leverage existing technical solutions as much as possible. We did have a challenging time succinctly explaining what the game actually

We want to make sure we can evolve with our players, so we will be focusing on things that help creations gain visibility and creators gaining notoriety.

was without showing it. The biggest thing we had to do was keep things moving very quickly to a prototype everyone could experience. This was paramount to getting the level of support we needed.

Q: How did you use your team approach to making sure the idea kept moving and happened?

A: The early days of the team consisted of only a very few team members. Their passion for Project Spark helped turn extremely daunting tasks that many would have, and did, tell us couldn't be done and weren't possible.

Q: How long did it take you from thinking about Project Spark to actually having a beta version on the market?

A: We started small and slowly ramped up, but it was about 3 years from the original idea to beta release.

Q: What were some of the resistances encountered and challenges along the way?

A: The biggest challenges were around scope, and being able to prove we could make something so grand and limitless to players within a realistic budget and timeframe. We were either breaking new ground or entering relatively new conventions on things all the time. New platforms, cross platform saving, touch controls, free to play, user generated content, rapid updates as a service, etc. All of these things presented their own challenges.

Q: As we all know, a first idea may change over time and have to be adapted. Talk to me about how you plan on keeping Project Spark alive and growing.

A: We've been working with an amazing community since our beta launched, and have been shaping the game to complete our vision while taking their desires and priorities into account. While there's always more features to add and things to do, immediately post-release we plan to focus on frequently introducing new content, features, and updates. We want to make sure we can evolve with our players, so we will be focusing on things that help creations gain visibility and creators gaining notoriety. There's several big things we'd like to do, but we plan to lock these plans down as we get closer to release.

BUILD YOUR BASE

"Life is not a solo act. It's a huge collaboration, and we all need to assemble around us the people who care about us and support us."

- Tim Gunn

I confess, I have a healthy ego, and I love when things are successful and I get credit for them. I have had really good successes in my life that reinforced my confidence in my abilities and my faith in my work. I believe I'm good at what I do, and that I have solid skills in my areas of expertise as a business performance consultant and leadership coach. I enjoy a fulfilling career, and have earned the respect of many people. I have made a difference in people's lives. I'm happy to know the world is a better place because I'm in it.

But there is a trap hidden in all of that written above. I can be lulled into thinking that I'm the one who has the answers. I'm the one who can lead this. That I know all of the answers, and that my ideas are all about me. It's the "Elizabeth Show." My interactions start to become more of me talking and less of me listening and learning. It becomes about me the leader and not about the value of the ideas I'm making happen.

To bring an idea to fruition, you may need to take a step back at times and remember that you're bringing an idea to fruition to provide value and enrich others through your idea. Enriching your life in many ways will happen too, but it shouldn't be the sole focus.

Do you remember back in Practice 3: Communicate, we talked about the non-profit board who lacked donors, volunteers, and members? One of the board member's family resented how much time he spent away working on the charity because they didn't understand what he was doing and why it was important. The conversation that came out of the inquiry resulted in a very hard look at why they had an exceptional idea of what they wanted to accomplish, but an absence of followers (donors and volunteers) to support it.

Any time you're lacking followers of your idea, the bottom line is, you didn't do one of the items listed below. You were not:

- Donor-centric (nonprofit world)

- Investor-centric (for-profit world)

- Community-centric (government or municipality world)

- Team-centric (project management world)

- Other-centric (catch-all term implying you have focus on others instead of yourself)

In other words, when you look at how you word, promote and sell your idea, if it's all about you, and what you do, and what you accomplish, and what you have, and how great you are, instead of how what you have and do enriches their lives and the lives of others, your approach will not build a strong team or base of followers for you. How do you build an other-centric culture that builds a following on your ideas? Here are some subtle ways to do it that will get your target audience excited, keep that audience involved, and constantly grow your fan base.

Step 1: Develop a Charity Model

A charity model is the concept that whatever your idea is, there is a component of the plan to share it in the world that benefits a charitable cause. An example is when someone launches a product and donates a portion of the sales to breast cancer. If you're a nonprofit leader reading this section, you're likely ahead of your for-profit peers on this one. For your target audience, you need to think about your idea, and how you can use that idea to give back to someone or something else. Research has proven that people will give preferential treatment and invest in those who are giving back in gratitude to charitable causes. There is an unselfish aspect to their vision and mission. You can look around the grocery store and see examples of charity models everywhere. This promotes both your brand or message—and theirs. This is a great win-win partnership in building your idea and a better world.

This step does not just apply to people with products to sell as part of their visions. Service providers can also give back a percentage of their profits, offer free seats or discounts to charity volunteers and employees, host charity fundraising events, promote a charity to their customers, and cross-brand. We do all of these programs at my company. I also donate portions of books sales to my clients' charities of choice when I speak at their events. It's a great thing to do for making the world a better place, and a fantastic way for moving your idea forward also.

Step 2: Embrace 'Co-opetition' not Competition

I do a lot of work with people in organizations around how their views on a particular issue may be limiting their Big Ideas moving forward. Many times, I can predict the results they're having without looking at a balance sheet or status report once I interview folks and ferret out the views people are holding. I worked with a charity client that provided environmental education. They were very upset at another organization they perceived as stealing their market share by offering very similar programs on the same topics. The relationship between the two organizations was declining. As you remember in Practice 3, we learned the following model:

I shared with them about how I used to live in a view of scarcity as a consultant. I had a view that if people were engaging in someone else's Big Idea, that it left less people to engage in mine. The actions that resulted out of this view were that I did not reach out, and I rarely partnered with anyone for fear they might steal my idea or customers. As a result, some of my most precious ideas stayed in small spaces and never got where I thought they should be for years until I shifted this view.

Then one day, I decided that the scarcity view was not working for me. I literally chose to hold a view of the world as an abundant place. Any decisions I made from that point forward were made assuming there is abundance for all. This does not mean my fear and the view of scarcity completely disappeared. I just made a very conscious decision that when that scarcity view came up, I would re-analyze the decision I thought I should make, and see how the choices I made would change by choosing to believe in an abundance of opportunity, money, partners, and/or resources. The outcome of that one small shift was having the best professional and personal relationships of my life, the most enjoyment I have ever experienced in my work, and vastly improved health and quality of life. So, I invited this non-profit organization to look at their views towards this other non-profit as competition and instead to look for all the ways they both could move forward together.

- I had them re-examine everything the organization offered in order to find the areas where they could form a partnership to increase impact

- I encouraged them to avoid competing in areas where the other organization clearly had better resources and products, looking at joint venturing and cross-promoting for mutual benefit (for example, selling their course as part of a local event that brought both organizations funding)

- Lastly, they could invite and use their experts and vice versa to be a part of each other's local events, to cooperate with that perceived competitor in ways that both benefit and grow 'co-opetition'

I got a call back a few days later and they were excited and enthused about all the possibilities this new business model opened up for them. In order to have co-opetition, it helps to come from a view of abundance, as I discussed earlier. It's important to realize that there are billions of people and dollars floating around in the world and no one idea, organization, or product has all those resources locked down in a monopoly. Coming up with models that bring everyone up, versus leaving the last man standing, are working everywhere. Just look at the number now of Internet millionaires. How do Brendon Burchard, Ryan Deiss, Frank Kern, Jeff Walker, and others gain money so quickly in such a crowded space? They have learned how to build their fan bases and leverage their competition into co-opetition.

In the modern marketplace, you'll see the principles of co-opetition applied most clearly in affiliate and joint venture partnerships. Affiliates are people who sell your products for a percentage of the sales. Joint ventures are relationships you can build with another organization where they specifically promote your product or service to their list of followers for a negotiated revenue share. The beauty of these types of agreements is that any organization can partner with another organization whether they're a business, charity, or government, to build their fan base even in realms where they look like they should be in competition. It also helps both organizations build their followers and fan base.

Definitions:

Affiliate Partnership - A partnership with organizations who will sell and promote your product, service, idea, or vision in return for a percentage of each sale they make. Amazon is a great example of an affiliate marketing program (e.g., if you sell product X, you get a specified percentage paid to you from the purchase price).

Joint Venture Partnership - A partnership with an organization that invests in you for some gain on the back end. They may promote your idea, product, service, or organization to their customers, or give you resources so you don't have to fund your product or service to get it on the market in return for a percentage of your profits on the back end. (Some organizations will even help you build your idea into a saleable product and then take a fixed percentage off the back end sales for a set period of time once you're in business.)

It's important to know that Idea Leaders and entrepreneurs in today's marketplace have to build quality relationships. These types of partnerships distinguish you to a target audience that may give you preference because of your partner vouching for you. They believe in you because of that relationship you have created with someone else who supports your idea. If you have affiliates and partners that vouch for you, your credibility, and impact, then your fan base has the opportunity to grow exponentially. Better to be in cooperation with your competitors in a way that you both win and grow your customer or fan bases.

Step 3: Become Customer-Centric

There is a subtle shift you'll need to make in your speaking and writing to truly be effective in your communications. I'm going to share two examples with you. See if you can spot the differences between them. (I have changed the names and numbers to protect the innocent.)

Example 1: BuildCorp Inc. is a nationally renowned leader in the building industry. Our award-winning designs and innovations have made us a recognized thought leader in the industry. Our mission is to ensure that green and healthy buildings are available to everyone. We have more than 50 local offices around the United States, more than 16,000 employees, and have completed more than 500 LEED-certified building projects. Our organization is a driving force in the building industry. We're a part of an industry that is projected to contribute $554 billion to the US gross domestic product in the next five years.

Example 2: The fulfillment of BuildCorp's mission is not driven through the buildings we design, but rather through the people who live and work in them. Our work empowers you, your organization, your friends, co-workers, and family to build healthy, affordable homes, offices and thriving community centers that promote your health. Thanks to your support of our business, we're able to work with professionals, teachers, politicians, administrators, government employees, and individuals like yourself to catalyze the revitalization of your community. Your support of our business allowed our employees to donate more than 1,000 hours educating local leaders and working in urban centers to ensure every person lives in a healthy, affordable home. Your repeat business and referrals have ensured the fulfillment of our mission—affordable, beautiful, healthy buildings for all.

Same company, vastly different copy. So, which of these BuildCorps would you prefer to support with your business? If you were in the market to build a home, which BuildCorps would you give your business to?

Looking back at the two examples, you probably would say that Example 1 is what we call a 'customer-optional' point of view. We did this, we did that, oh how amazing we are. Look at everything they've done. It's all we we we and us us us...

Now after reading Example 2, you can see that it's clearly from the customer-CENTRIC point of view. They realize that without their investors and customers, they would not be where they are today. They credit you for their successes. They say subtly how you can continue to keep them successful. They also stress their charity model. They simply share their vision.

And finally they stress that without your help, they wouldn't have been (and won't be) as successful in the future. It's all YOU YOU YOU. How did that feel for you personally when you read it? Did you feel good about yourself and how they were impacting your community?

Now, when I write, I always review it from the customer's point of view. I play my own devil's advocate and ask, "Why me, why now, and why you?" I will also circle every time I say 'you' and underline everywhere I get into the we/me mode. Then I re-write it from the customer's point of view and what they would care about (thank you, Tom Ahern, for teaching me the Circle the You practice many years ago when I was learning fundraising!). This is a simple, subtle shift you can make in how you communicate your idea, your product, and your service, and make big gains in your fan base. Just look at how many you's I got into that last sentence!

Step 4: Make the big, small

There is a problem with Big Ideas. The reason they're often called BHAGs—Big Hairy Audacious Goals—is that they can be so big, your target audience can't see how their contribution will get you to that endpoint. To illustrate this point, let's look at 'Making the big, small' from an investor's point of view.

INVESTOR CASE STUDY:

Proposal to Invest Capital into an Idea Funding a Leadership Education Product Targeted for use in Public School Systems.

Company A has an idea. They want to sell curricula that teaches kids to be leaders to every public school system in the United States. To an investor who wants to invest $100,000, the public school system is a huge, perplexing mess of thousands of individual bureaucracies, overlaid by state and federal bureaucracies, yielding a very risky, cumbersome curricula-approval process and interactions with feisty boards made up of local citizens. How the heck will Company A ever get a cutting-edge leadership curricula into every public school system in the nation? How long could it take before investors ever saw a return on their investment?

Answer: Company A would do best to focus on telling the story of how they will get the curricula into one major and influential school system. Then, explain how they'll leverage that success across the nation's school system one school system at a time. The investor can see that there is the process, predict the time it will take to yield a profit on the first phase, and see how their $100,000 investment will grow from that point forward.

NONPROFIT DONOR CASE STUDY:

Proposal To Fund Training For Teachers On How To Maintain A Healthy, Germ-Free School Environment.

Nonprofit B needs $1,000 per school in order to train teachers to maintain a healthy, germ-free school environment. But, their average donation is only $50. Nonprofit B could appeal to their donors and say, "We need $1,000 per school and here is why it takes $1,000." They may get to their funding goal eventually, but would have to run a repeated and powerful campaign of measuring and pushing people toward a goal in this approach. How could they get there faster by 'making the big, small'?

Answer: Break it down to something they can relate to and state specifically how their donation contributes to the $1,000 total so people feel their donation results in an immediate shift for the school.

It costs $1,000 to train our teachers and staff how to create a healthy school. How does your $50 donation make the difference today?

**$50 provides 10 classroom toolkits and study guides

**$50 can purchase an air monitor that the students

---

can use to complete healthy classroom projects and improve air quality across the entire school

**$50 will pay for the transportation costs to allow a teacher or administrator to attend our workshop and become a certified "Healthy School Administrator"

It does not take much to have an immediate impact right now on the health of a child. Your gift of $50 will make a difference today.

As you can see in the previous examples, when you take that big vision and break it down into actionable pieces, you can have more success in building your fan base and your fundraising base!

Step 5: Appeal to your Whole Customer

There are marketing firms that employ experts who can educate you on the psychology behind effective communication and branding. You could work with different firms and get multiple unique and different opinions on the most effective way to appeal to your whole customer.

If we're boot-strapping our own idea into reality, our only resource may be what we can afford to read or learn on the Internet. The good news is that there are some basic tried-and-true ways to get the attention of an investor, donor, customer, co-worker or whomever else you need to engage.

Therefore, when you want to engage your fan base, remember the following mantra:

- I'm emotional. I'm skeptical. Surprise me. Make me feel special. Make it easy on me.

When these different personalities I list in my mantra above hear a pitch, the following is what they're secretly thinking:

The Emotional Me

I love a good story. I love belonging and being a part of something. I love to share my emotions and excitement with others. I love being connected.

The Skeptical Me

What are you trying to trick me into? This can't possibly work. Who are you and why should I trust you? Until you prove to me that you aren't out to rip me off, you are.

The Exciting Me

I'm part of the technology revolution. I'm bombarded every day. Please tell me something I don't know. Give me different, unique. Surprise me! Make me feel the urgency. Make me feel the excitement.

The VIP Me

I want to know that working with you makes me, too, special and unique. I feel important. I have stake in this. I'm a VIP. You value me.

The Action Me

Where are you going with this? What do I need to do next? How fast and easy will it be for me to do it? I am ready. Go, and make it quick. Don't slow me down. I'm a busy person.

If you want to grab each of the five 'me' personalities, to ensure each becomes a part of your fan base, the following are a few tips to engage them.

How to Appeal to the Emotional Me

Faces and eye contact: The simplest way to engage the emotional me is to ensure that whatever you do with me includes faces and eye contact. Psychologists around the world have done all sorts of tests showing that, given a choice between a picture of a building or a picture of a person looking at you in front of a building, the larger majority of people gravitate to the person. The use of children and pets can increase this phenomenon significantly, as we have something in our psychology that wires us to focus on kids and animals.

Next time you walk through the grocery store checkout line, notice how many magazine covers have people looking right at you. See if you notice those magazines first. This also applies in person and on video. Look at people, and they will be engaged. Look away and you lose their interest, and possibly their trust. Remember what your dad said about people who couldn't look you in the eye?

Anecdotes and stories: We love a good story. We love things that excite and stimulate our imagination. We love things that paint a picture for us. Tell your story. Tell other's stories. It creates connectedness, engagement and investment. At the beginning of this book, I shared my personal story with you so that you would know who I am and why I wrote this book. Many of you could probably relate to something I shared in that story. It made this Big Idea concept real. It set the tone as conversational vs. formal.

To see how these tips could apply to you, take a look at something you have recently presented or written. Are you using anecdotes to illuminate the most pressing things? Are you aiming for the heart? Have you included emotional triggers: hope, fear, peace, anger, generosity, greed, exclusivity, abundance, scarcity, opportunity, and urgency?

Here is an example of storytelling I wrote that I used for a local chapter that was working to promote healthy, green schools via the Parent-Teacher Association (PTA).

Educational Flyer Promoting an Event - What is a Green School?

Imagine your children walking into a school where everything they see and touch teaches them a life lesson. From the desk they sit in, to the air they breathe, to the materials the building is made from, to the food they eat. They know the impacts of building on the environment, their money, and their health because they experience it every day. Welcome. Your children have just spent a day in a living, learning laboratory we call a green school!

Now, there is nothing technically wrong with giving facts and data, but it will only appeal to a very limited audience called 'the choir,' as most people don't even know what *green school* means. This chapter I worked with was reaching out to people who had never heard of a green school. The text engages the emotions and the senses. It appeals to the Emotional Me. The Emotional Me doesn't have to become 'the choir' or know all the facts to engage. They will support and engage because you connected to something that resonated with their deepest self.

How to Appeal to The Skeptical Me

The number one way to appeal to the Skeptical Me is by using testimonials. The Skeptical Me wants to know actual people who

Make it a habit to collect testimonials from everyone.

vouch that you are who you say you are, or that your idea, product or services are as good as you say they are, or that your organization makes the difference you claim it makes. Make it a habit to collect testimonials from everyone—even anonymous ones that just list first name and city/state. The beauty of testimonials is that they work on the macro-scale, where you are selling on a big stage, to the micro-scale, where you may just be getting a group of co-workers to support you in a new initiative or idea. Having some other person say, "Yes, I support this—and this is why," gives you credibility. Never walk into a meeting alone when you can walk in with an ally. Adopt this practice and see your fan base grow.

Sample Testimonial: We're very pleased to collaborate with such a great organization. Awesome Training Company Inc.'s education opportunities are unmatched in developing the leaders our company wants to hire. We look forward to our continued relationship! Dennis Quinton, President of XYZ Restaurant Association, Greensboro, NC.

Testimonials help you battle back the skeptical mind which is saying: This is a waste of my money or time, or it's too expensive. This organization or person really won't deliver what

> **People like to be shocked and surprised. It gives a psychological jolt to learn something that changes their current views of what is so.**

they say because it's hard for me to believe it at face value. Who made them the expert? Maybe they won't be here next year. Who else is doing this same thing only better/cheaper/bigger?

How to appeal to The Exciting Me

Who doesn't love the thrill of being the first to know, the first to have an opportunity, the first in line at the door? In this world where you're bombarded with blah blah blah all day long, doesn't it feel good when someone genuinely takes you by surprise and you learn something, feel something, or get to experience something out of the ordinary? Keep surprising your fan base and they will stay engaged. How do you surprise people? Are you telling (and showing) people things they don't know? Does your information have news value? Is it unique and innovative? Are your photos surprising in some way?

Some tried-and-true tactics include:

Ask a question that they will keep reading or listening to in order to find the answer. We're curious by nature, particularly if you ask a question that challenges a view that is commonly accepted as truth. Trivia questions also work, as well as polls and surveys, as they can see how people are voting on a topic in real time. Check out the example here on fresh organic food versus grocery store produce.

Did you know that it costs less to eat local and organic than from a grocery store?

That will surprise most people, because the current perception is that organic food is more expensive. This farmer's market can then expound on why they're cheaper, and drive business to their farmer's market.

Make a statement that flies in the face of an accepted view. As in the example above about organic foods, there are many things people just accept as true. If you can show that your idea delivers something else, something they care about, something that solves a problem, something that makes their life better, something that adds joy and fun to their day, you may get their attention.

Mommy, I'm bummed it's Saturday because I really want to go to school!

This public charter school then revealed the statistic that the students who attend their school love it so much, they ask their parents if they can go on Saturday. They talk about how their school is designed to be a living, learning laboratory so that kids don't want to leave because of all the cool ways they learn, thus making their school unique.

Tell me something surprising. People like to be shocked and surprised. It gives a psychological jolt to learn something that changes their current views of what is so. Think about your idea and the difference it could make in the world. Many ideas change the entire cultural perception of what is possible when the idea comes to fruition. Take time to look around for things that would surprise and delight your fan base. See where you can connect your work to a news story, trend, or meme. Give them access to something happening 'live' and right now.

Did you know that people who never own cars save $100,000 more dollars over their lifetime than people who do?

This sounds shocking, and might be useful for a company that was trying to encourage people to give up their cars and use their bike rental and hourly car rental transportation service.

How to appeal to The VIP Me

The VIP Me wants to know that you value "me, my time, and my contribution." I want to feel special. I'm not just a face in the crowd. My association with you, your company, your product, or your mission sets me apart from the crowd. So how should you appeal to The VIP Me?

Make them privy to something previously unknown to them. Send them a piece of news that would appeal to them because they care or are interested in a certain thing. For example, if you were targeting budget-conscious shoppers, sending them shopping tips like, "Did you know that shopping on Mondays ensures that you get the best selection of items that are on sale for that week?"

Give them a sneak peak and a daring new person, program, product or initiative to engage in. Let them know they're now in the know.

Example: Launching an idea for a life-changing medical device

Email/Teaser, Social Media post: Your veteran's life could change on October 1. Disabled veterans who have been house-confined since their injury will be free to live, work, and play thanks to the launch of a revolutionary new medical device.

This statement would be followed with an article about a new medical device that allows people with ileostomies and colostomies who have had to quit their jobs, are unable to do housework, or even pick up and hug their kids to resume normal activities. Millions of Americans will be freed as a result of this new technology, and these people heard it first from you and may impact people they know.

Give them VIP Access. Give them advance notice of something, or a deal on something just for them. Give them free tickets to events, free information, or education. Recognize them publicly. Provide behind-the-scenes access opportunities for a meet and greet. Introduce them to people they might not ordinarily meet. Give them rewards, benefits, and incentives for their support, like free or discounted memberships. Have member cards that, when they use them or show them, they get special benefits with your or in their local community. Have events or meetings just for them.

How to appeal to The Action Me

The Action Me is a busy person. They don't have the time. They hate to waste time. They're not giving you their full attention. If you have successfully appealed to the other 'me' personalities, this 'me' is ready to act.

- Is whatever you have given them a complete and quick read?

- Are you using short sentences, action verbs, and NO JARGON? Jargon is word or acronym you use that would not be understood by everyone reading it.

- Is it easy for skimmers, flippers, and browsers to glean the necessary information?

- Do the headlines and pictures give the key messages?

- Are you using statistics like an arrow to make a single important point to drive them to action?

- Most importantly, have you made at least one clear offer they can respond to?

- Is it clear how to respond to your offer?

- Is it easy to respond, (i.e. you have tested it)? It's simple. No special steps. Minimal inconvenience.

Answer those questions 'yes' and you have The Action Me in a happy place!

Steps 1 through 5 all lead to this final step. When you understand the first five steps and can form them into a cohesive plan, the outcome is called relationship fundraising.

Step 6: Develop a Relationship Fundraising Plan

What is relationship fundraising? In this book, I want to be clear that I am using the term to apply to all realms of building your fan base: public, private, for-profit, government, and charity. No matter what type of business you're in, this is, in my opinion, the most effective way to manage your idea partners and build your fan base, as well as (if needed) raise money for your idea.

I define fundraising more broadly than the traditional terminology, to include: money, time, expertise, and resources. All of these are needed to make your idea happen. The goal of building your fan base is to get people to give you more than just money. You want to build a relationship with them that lasts.

Fundraising is everything you do, and all your activities that result in getting the resources you need to implement your idea, including money, time, materials, expertise, and any other tangible commodity. These are the critical resources you need that allow your idea to move forward.

Relationship fundraising is having a fundraising strategy where your idea centers on the unique and special relationship between you and each customer or supporter. Your overriding consideration is to care for and develop that bond and to do nothing through your idea creation process that might damage or jeopardize that relationship.

In the world of moving an idea from thought to reality, all of your marketing activity is geared toward making sure your customer (investor, donor, partner, volunteer, co-worker, friend, family) know he or she is important, valued, and considered. This has the effect of maximizing support and funds you'll receive from that person in the long term. You're focused on what the customer wants to buy from your idea and what they value versus what you want to sell. All customers are acknowledged, no matter how small their contribution.

I am not a big fan of long, complex plans. If they go more than a few pages, I won't use them. So keep in mind that the two-step outline I'm giving you in this practice should not become a 100-page tome on your computer or on your desk. It should always be short, sweet, and actionable.

Define your base

Your first step will be to define your fan base. Who do you need to reach and keep engaged to see your idea happen? This can be broad categories like investor, customer, affiliates, joint-venture partners, charity model partner for big projects, or it can be a listing of people for team member roles for local or internal initiatives.

Map out how you will be in relationship with them

Your second step is to answer the following set of questions for each fan base category (parents, engineers, school teachers):

- What is their role in my vision implementation?

- What resource will they provide me?

- What do they want to buy from me/my idea?

- By what methods will I reach them?

- How will they communicate back to me if they want to?

- How often should I be in contact with them?

- How often will I seek their input or opinion formally (i.e., my feedback loop)?

- What do they need or want to know ongoing?

- How will I keep them engaged?

- How will I thank them?

- If applicable, how will I move them to the next level of fundraising commitment?

If what you wrote is very specific, clear, and actionable for each fan, you can use it to build your fundraising calendar and relationship management system discussed in Step 7.

Step 7: Manage Your Relationships

As I mentioned in Step 5, I considered myself in my early career to be a good rainmaker, but not a great one. Some may argue that raising a million dollars makes you a great fundraiser for a company. I would argue back that if you raised 1 million dollars for a company that is good. But, if you could have raised 5 million dollars if you had just properly managed your relationships, suddenly that 1 million dollars looks good, but definitely not great.

To be frank, in the past, I left money on the table. Although I mastered taking care of my existing clients on each project, I failed to leverage the additional value I had to offer, and leverage their loyalty and referrals they could have given me. Once the project was done, I let the relationship go until they called me again. All this relationship capital was left on the table because, as an engineer, I perceived it wrong to be a sales and marketing person and sell the real value I was offering.

In reality, if I had embraced the concept of relationship fundraising, I could have exponentially expanded my business years before I actually did, and in a way that benefitted everyone. I loved meeting and working with people. I truly love and respect all of my clients and enjoy my time with them. At the end of the day, people buy from people.

Very few relationships in life are no maintenance. Every relationship needs some time and attention or it fades away. I am a big believer now of tracking, cataloguing and managing every relationship I make, whether it's a short encounter, personal, professional, or through my social media channels. In these relationships, I have discovered a gold mine of resources for any and all ideas I come up with. When I started tracking

> **Very few relationships in life are no maintenance. Every relationship needs some time and attention or it fades away.**

all the relationships I had, I was shocked to see that the number of people I knew and could reach out to was in the thousands just in my personal contacts; that didn't include their network of contacts. Yet, I was actively taking care of about 200 of those people; but those 200 people had 15 million contacts who could benefit from my ideas that I did nothing about for years.

No matter which system you choose, it's worth your time AND money to get everyone into a customer relationship management (CRM) system. Even if you just get everyone into an Excel spreadsheet and have tabs to keep them in groups, it would be a great start. There are many affordable tools to scan in business cards quickly, use your smartphone to pull them into programs like Evernote or Scanbiz, and of course there are a plethora of CRM programs online that can let you email personally and touch base with people in your network with ease like NationBuilder, Salesforce, and MailChimp. I am a huge fan of LinkedIn to manage relationships because it's professional, and really designed to build a business. It's also an extremely underutilized resource by most people. The good news is that there are so many affordable options out there.

Why should you use a customer relationship management system?

Setting up and maintaining a complete relationship database enables you to keep track of all of your communications with everyone. If you're working across a large group who are your target audience(s), it can also let you know who knows whom, and who is contacting whom.

Your goal in Step 6 was to create a Relationship Fundraising Plan, including a calendar that systemizes building and maintaining your relationships. The fan base categories you came up with in Step 6 will be a start to creating categories of relationships you can manage in your CRM. You can slice and dice them however you want, and some people may be in multiple groups (which you can tag them for in a CRM):

Investor	Customer	Co-workers	Family
Affiliates	Joint Venture Partners	Friends	Clients
Volunteers	Potential Customers	Resources	Expertise
Donors	Past Customers	Staff	Marketing

You can create groups as unique as your idea. Start looking at every relationship and every possible way each might support you in your idea. As you launch more ideas, you can see that some people can support all different types of ideas you come up with. If you're going to design a great fitness program for overweight dogs, suddenly you might have a group called 'dog owners' and manage them appropriately. That includes people who might be your friends, co-workers, or neighbors.

Become the Customer

You don't need to have a degree in psychology or be a guru marketer to figure out how to manage most of these relationships. Just take the time to place yourself in their shoes—and views. If you were the target audience, how would you like to be treated? Thanked? Worked with? Informed? What would you like as incentives? What would inspire you to do more?

Second, think about their views in general. If you want a certain result from them, what views would they need to adopt, or commitment would they need to make to take the action that produces the result you want? For example, if you have an idea to get more people to work from home one or more days per week, then their manager might have to adopt a view that working from home was valuable, or commit to letting you start a pilot program to get it moving.

Repeat Over and Over: Thank, acknowledge, incentivize

Remember that relationship building begins the moment the person chooses to become engaged in your idea. Time matters in thanking. You should be thanking and acknowledging their connection to you/your idea within 48 hours. I thank everyone as quickly as possible, even if it's just a short e-mail, and set a goal to do so in fewer than 48 hours at the most, when people fund any aspect of my various businesses whether they're donating time, buying a service, or providing a resource.

Many Idea Leaders will tell you that the biggest challenge to keeping people on board with your idea is to get them to invest again and to invest more. Same goes for customers. Thanking often and providing incentives works, and it can be simple. Just an e-mail or personal note can be enough. Or, you can send them a coupon, offer them a free tool/gift, invite them to an event, provide them with a useful resource, or connect them to someone. Remember the old adage, "You never get a second chance to make a first impression." So, make the first impression a sincere 'thank you.'

What comes after the thank you?

Your target audience will want to know that their money was set to work as intended and what the outcomes were. They may like to be recognized somehow, but not necessarily singled out or thanked publicly. I find it's helpful if you're not sure where they sit on recognition to just ask, "I would like to mention you at this event or include you in this e-mail, is that okay?"

Whether you're working with an investor, customer, or donor, remember that you should take way more time to keep them informed than to ask them for more money, sales, or resources. It can be hard when you get started to master this practice, so automate it as much as possible with the technologies that are out there. And also make sure that you know for each target audience how often you'll contact them and how the contact will happen.

The more you can do to make your investors, donors, team members, customers and experts see themselves as partners and supporting a common goal, the better. When tracking idea investors, I consider time as valuable as money and resources. I will assign a monetary value to their contribution just like it was cash, and manage the relationship and acknowledge their contribution based on that amount. For example, let's say that I have a client who provides me a free training venue for my public events, which saves me thousands of dollars every year. Therefore, I manage that relationship differently than someone who is just on my mailing list. I often offer them extra services at no charge as a thank you for supporting the work that I do.

Steps to Success - Making your Big Idea Happen Right Now!

To build a strong fan base around your idea, you need to:

- Build a charity model around your vision

- Embrace 'co-opetition' not competition

- Become customer-centric

- Make the big things appear small

- Appeal to the whole person by touching the 5 Me's (Emotional, Skeptical, Exciting, VIP, and Action Me)

- Develop a relationship fundraising plan

- Make relationship management the way you do business

To master this practice, put yourself on a *12-week Building Your Fan Base Plan*. If you have shorter time scale to do this, you can pull the schedule in; but if you have a longer time scale, continue to manage yourself to 12 weeks so you make progress.

Week 1

Spend 15 minutes daily gathering every relationship you have. These can come from phonebooks, business cards, and contacts on your cell phone, social media, family, and church.

Week 2

See who you already have in your network to help on the idea, and identify who you need to find and add.

Week 3

Think about your idea and see what charity model might make sense for what you're doing. Write it down.

Week 4

Who do you view as competition for what you want to do? Decide how you could leverage them as co-opetition not competition.

Week 5

Pull out your written materials and your OM³. Does it pass the 'you' test? Is it customer-centric? Is your big vision explained in a way that is easy to digest and see the small steps to get to the big outcome?

Week 6-8

Develop a plan to appeal to the 5 Me's for each key person(s) or group of persons as part of your relationship fundraising plan.

Week 9-12

Take everything above and now systematize it. Make it part of how you work your vision.

SUCCESS STORIES FROM IDEA LEADERS

Dr. Kieren Kuykendall, D.C., Founder, The Applied Kinesiology Center

Some ideas come to us during the darkest circumstances. Dr. Kuykendall used his own personal health battles with debilitating illness and lack of support from traditional medical establishments to inspire him to become a doctor and create a one-of-a-kind treatment center for people who have been told there is nothing that can be done for their chronic health issues. Dr. Kuykendall uses a cutting edge formula that looks at the four primary causes of ill health: structural issues, nutritional imbalances, emotional blockages and toxicity. His approaches are simple and life-changing for his patients. His process had made it easy and understandable for patients to become empowered and to unlock their own human health potential and heal their bodies!

Q: What idea or thought came into your head that helped you create The Applied Kinesiology Center?

> Someone offered me a lifeline at a time when I was in complete and total darkness just made me fall in love with my career path. I decided this is what I want to do for other people. It feeds me to give my heart every day.

A: Purpose out of pain is what I call it. It was a purpose out of pain experience, where I went through a lot of pain and I was very sick. I was very desperate, and going to doctors and I couldn't get better. No matter what I tried, I couldn't get better. Somebody told me 'I know this guy. He's a great doctor and he's a chiropractor. I thought at the time, *why would I be going to a chiropractor?* They just know about backs, right? I didn't have back pain.

But, I was desperate, and I had fibromyalgia and pain and I was very, very sick. I was in bed for two years. I went to see this guy, and he actually shared his heart with me, got down on his knees and prayed for me. He showed me he was very sincere and very committed to really being there with me through the process. This was his mission.

Having someone offered me a lifeline at a time when I was in complete and total darkness just made me fall in love with my career path. I decided this is what I want to do for other people. It feeds me to give my heart every day.

Q: So it sounds like you had a desire to be of deep service and really support people in a deeper way than allowed in traditional medicine?

A: There is nothing more amazing than what I get to do. Recently, I have been working with a woman who is having pain, who can't get pregnant, who is being told terrible things by her doctors, and she's desperate. I helped her eliminate all those things, and then she was able to get pregnant. She and her family were able to have the baby.

I had one lady who had lost six babies late term, who came to see me after seeing fertility doctors. She was having terrible breast pain and afraid she had breast cancer. I told her this is different, and you're working on a whole other playing field now. I told her, "Your body is healthier." She is eight or nine months along in a pregnancy, and I was able to help her with the process. I told her, "You have totally changed your whole body, your whole system." Understandably, she was dealing with the emotional stress of possibly losing this baby late term. So, we went through and started doing some of the emotional work that we do. She had the baby. She's brought the baby in and I have worked on the baby. And what's amazing is that one day I will work on that baby's children. The people who come in to see me are like family to me. It's really a beautiful thing.

Q: Where do you get the energy to keep going when you have frustrations or resistance?

A: For me it's being invested in where my patients' lives are headed. There is no separation between me and them. Every person who comes in mirrors me; my fears, my concerns, my love, my passion, and my desires. We're all the same. We just look different. It's all an illusion. That really feeds me, getting to the core of it. Watching people transform, sharing the excitement with them, it's really beautiful.

Q: How did you train to do this? What was the path you had to take to get there with your commitment to this idea of being a different type of doctor?

A: It takes a total desire to truly want to help people transform their lives. Thank God it was really my passion, because otherwise it would have been brutal. For me it was the passion of really wanting to achieve the goal of transforming people's lives. I can't think of anything more sacred. Like the purpose-driven life. I can't think of anything I would rather do, that would be more sacred and more amazing to help the world. I can help a woman who is a teacher, and she can go out there and shift children's lives. It was that passion, that love, that desire for the goal that kept me moving. I also truly love learning this stuff.

Q: When you talk about learning, what did you have to do to be taught all these specialties that you do?

A: Obviously there is the medical piece, where I was learning all the blood chemistry, all the hormones and all of the nutritional stuff. Then there was all the personal development. I

> Everyone has the same fears and pain, and when you really connect with people at that human level, you'll do anything to help them.

traveled to the Amazon and spent time with Indian tribes and natives living in the Andes Mountains. It radically changed the way I perceive the world. It's a true life experience of people just being humans.

It was not just learning the medical part, but learning the part in my life where I connect with people. It was learning to connect with people at the heart level for me. Everyone has the same fears and pain, and when you really connect with people at that human level, you'll do anything to help them.

Q: When you decided to make this shift to a non-traditional practice, what were all the little voices in your head that you had to deal with?

A: First of all, it's the human condition to have that 'voice'; it never stops. Every time you get to the next level, there is always going to be new voices, either yours or other people's, that are going to try to stop you or slow you down. Basically it's my cultural training, my socio-economic training, and my ego training from the society we live in that tell us the way things should or should not be. I realized it wasn't my path to live the standard life, because it wasn't me being fully self-expressed. I just don't listen to the voices anymore.

Q: What advice would you give to someone who is waiting to make their idea happen?

A: I like the saying, begin before you're ready. I began practicing new things I learned before I was ready and I had a lot of voices going on like, *Do I know enough? Do I have anything important to say? Will people listen to me? Will people resonate to me?* So getting a training on the books and saying, okay, I am going to go take the training and then when I get back Monday morning I am going to do some of this stuff with people and see how they respond. It was starting to chip away at it, but just trusting your inner knowing that you have something really powerful and really valuable to offer the world.

Q: It sounds like you were able to overcome your resistance and fear to trying new things.

A: Yes, it's really getting in the heart space. Always give love and gratitude to people, whether they're in anger, whether they're in happiness, or in frustration. To just love and appreciate other people for where they are in their human experience. One, it will help them heal, and two, it will help me be a better doctor

> **Always give love and gratitude to people, whether they're in anger, whether they're in happiness, or in frustration.**

and a better business person, because my heart's in it for them. I can move through difficult circumstances because I am always coming from a space of love and gratitude.

Q: One of the things I have noticed when I'm working with people on making an idea happen is that the people who are really successful have a knack for surrounding themselves with teams of support and structures that keep them on the path. How did you figure out that support structure?

A: I built my support by going to the places I love to be. I love learning. I love nature. I love spiritual groups. Whenever you're vibrating at your highest level, those people are also vibrating at those levels, and they show up; and it's effortless. You have new patients come in to see you that you met at the weekend workshop, and you have this amazing new team and this amazing person who shows up. They're there to work with you and get you to the next level and you didn't even know it, but they were right there in front of you the whole time.

Q: What were your fears in moving this idea forward?

A: The lack of value in what I was doing, worrying about if I am valuable or do I have something that will help people. My biggest enemy was myself and my own self-doubt.

Q: How did you move through that fear?

A: It was mainly just working on my love and gratitude for myself, and stepping back and taking a moment for myself. Stepping back and seeing the forest for

> One hundred percent follow your heart without a doubt, because if it's in your heart, that is the truest vibration, and the other stuff is all story.

the trees, and being able to see where you're at. Knowing and remembering what my mission on earth is. Looking at my mission statement is helpful. It's really to awaken and inspire people to greatness. Really trusting my inner knowing. I know it in my heart, therefore it is. Meditation and trusting myself kept me grounded.

Q: If someone felt like they had a Big Idea and a calling and something they wanted to go for, what advice would you give them?

A: One hundred percent follow your heart without a doubt, because if it's in your heart, that is the truest vibration, and the other stuff is all story. It's all secondary and just thoughts, emotions, feelings. It's what is really in your heart that you have to follow.

TAKING YOUR IDEA FROM MISSION TO MILLION$

"We can't solve problems by using the same kind of thinking we used when we created them."

- Albert Einstein

When I came up with the framework for this book, I was very intentional in creating a set of practices that were scalable and adaptable to ideas big and small. Whether someone wants to work locally in their neighborhood with a few friends, start a non-profit that solves a big societal problem, or a business has an idea to develop a product they want to make millions of dollars from, the practices apply and scale up or down.

The book was also created with a strong awareness on my part to the wisdom Albert Einstein imparted in the quote gracing this epilogue. What he stated simply and brilliantly, was 'we cannot get there from here.' So, this book also intentionally captures your idea wherever it births from in your mind or your life. Then, the practices very deliberately pull you out of that context from which you birthed your idea and into a different set of contexts, to be sure the problems that were behind that original idea don't stop you from being successful in making that idea happen.

Take Daily Action

From this day forward, you now have your *Mission to Million$ Journal.* You're on a mission to fulfill your ideas. Every day, you will set aside 5–15 minutes of time to journal the actions you will take on your goals each day. Journaling is best typically first thing in the morning, or before you go to bed at night. As you get more practice, you'll notice you journal throughout day as the wind shifts and different actions are required.

I have a personal commitment to take at least five minutes of action each day on my Big Ideas. **A good question to ask yourself each morning or evening is,** *What is one thing I could do today to make progress on the idea?* I promise you that after working with and interviewing dozens of Idea Leaders, their daily actions don't include constantly responding to everything that comes in via LinkedIn, Twitter, Facebook, e-mail, phone, or text. The next thing you know, your entire day is gone.

Don't stop making progress by focusing on big items that take hours to complete. **Small actions producing wins are important to grow your energy and confidence!** Look at something you can do in the short-term.

- Make a phone call

- Study something on the Internet

- Sign up for a course

- Have a short conversation about the idea

- Ask someone questions about the idea

- Attend a meeting and network

- Call someone and share the idea

- Read something relevant to your idea

- Meet a new person

- Meditate

- Write tomorrow's actions up

As you complete the day's actions, check them off and celebrate. If you don't complete them that day, don't make yourself wrong. Instead, keep them live, attack it again the next day, and check them off whenever they get done. Small steps every day make for big outcomes.

What If I Feel Like I'm Stuck?

When I work with my clients on their ideas and they feel stuck, I ask them, "What actions did you write to be accomplished today?" Many times I find they decided to skip a day, then two days. Next thing you know a week has gone by, and no progress has been made. Focus is lost. Blurry vision sets in. If you go long enough, idea death happens as you start talking yourself into the impossibility of what you're doing.

Daily actions help you see things are moving and getting done on the way to the Big Idea. Taking your commitments and writing goals also helps you to create a solid strategy to achieve the Big Idea. Without your goals and daily actions driving your idea roadmap, you and your idea will get lost.

What if I'm Failing?

Any time you feel that failure conversation creeping in, don't go there. Instead, focus on what actions would someone who is succeeding at this idea take, and write them down in your daily action journal. There is no inspiration or action in focusing on failures.

> I believe life is constantly testing us for our level of commitment and life's greatest rewards are reserved for those who demonstrate a never-ending commitment to act until they achieve. As simple as this may sound, it's still the common denominator separating those who live their dreams from those who live in regret.
>
> - Anthony Robbins

So make the commitment right now. Take that shot. Start today, as soon as you close this book. Your idea is that close to happening for you.

"You miss every shot that you don't take."

- Wayne Gretzky

Thank you for taking the time to read this book. I am well aware that we only have so much time on this earth, and you just spent some of that life energy with me. I'm honored, and I look forward to hearing what you have accomplished on my blog, *Mission Accomplished* at www. missiontomillionsbook.com/blog.

Are you ready to take a step further into leadership and thought mastery? Do you want to be more effective at managing yourself and others to change yourself and thus change the world?

Pre-order Book 2: *Change Yourself. Change Others.*

Available for Pre-order September 20, 2014

Synopsis: It's so easy to judge others. Why can't they change this? Why don't they see that? We spend a lot of life energy working to change others, whether they're our spouse, our kids, our friends, our bosses, or our co-workers. Most of us miss the fact that we ourselves can't even change our own behaviors, so how can we expect others to change so easily?

Book 2 of the Empowering People Into Leadership Series, *Change Yourself. Change Others* focuses on understanding why you don't change, and teaches powerful practices to master changing your own behavior. By mastering these techniques, you can start to powerfully shift your own behavior, and master your own circle of influence. One you change yourself, you'll be able to see where others are stuck in their own behaviors, and guide them to another possibility of action.